Advance Praise for *Disrupted*

"The most effective 'Working Together'™ leaders create a psychologically safe environment where everyone can share the truth—green, yellow, or red—so the team can work together effectively and efficiently including all of the stakeholders. *Disrupted* provides leaders with practical tools to do exactly that, while staying positive and focused. Andre W. Thornton has written a clear, human-centered system that helps leaders and teams turn disruption into learning, alignment, and outstanding outcomes."
—**Alan Mulally**, Former CEO of Boeing and Ford

"*Disrupted* hits the nail on the head. Its methodical approach displaces fear of the unknown with confidence in chaos. I will keep this book within reach as a daily resource."
—**Robert M. Wise**, Entrepreneur, Founder, and CEO

"In complex organizations, disruption doesn't just test strategy; it tests leadership behavior at scale. I've seen Andre's approach in action with my own teams, and it drives clarity, alignment, and stronger execution under pressure. *Disrupted* bridges human performance and business results in a way that is practical, disciplined, and immediately applicable for leaders navigating enterprise-level change."
—**Ruth O. Davis**, Director and Client Partner, IBM Consulting

"Are you tired of operating out of fear? Wondering how to handle the constant disruption and changes of life? This book helps you consistently turn lemons into lemonade. As a lifelong builder and transformationalist who lives in Thornton's 'Adaptable' quadrant, it has been a joy to see his personal transformation as a 'People Engineer'—helping others and now sharing those tangible frameworks, tools, and mindset with an even broader audience."
—**Gerald Charles Jr.**, SVP and Chief Information Officer, Coca-Cola Beverages Florida

"*Disrupted* is the much-needed leader's guide in our new world of constant change and chaos."
—**Karna Crawford**, Former Head of US Marketing, Ford Motor Company

"*Disrupted* offers a disciplined, human-centered framework for increasing agility and turning volatility into velocity—exactly the leadership muscle required in today's environment."
—**Erica Cary**, Global HR Executive

"I've known Andre W. Thornton for over fifteen years, since we met during leadership training with The Executive Leadership Council in 2010. *Disrupted* reflects the thoughtful, disciplined leadership I've seen in him throughout his journey—from aerospace engineer at Lockheed Martin to trusted advisor with the founding of Whitman Consulting. Blending personal experience with practical tools, Thornton provides a clear framework for navigating disruption: understanding what happened, managing yourself, and leading others through change. A powerful and practical guide that helps readers transform disruption into clarity, resilience, and lasting growth."
—**Javara Perrilliat**, President, West Division, QXO

"Thornton has captured in writing what I experienced with him in hours of in-person coaching. He delivers to the page insights built on his unique combination of personal life disruptions, his passion for both the art and science of people, and just enough engineering (and football) discipline to break it all down into concise frameworks and personal calls to introspection. His unique lived experience and ability to frame repeatable, proven methods from inside an engineer's mind ensures that *Disrupted* is both insightful and actionable."
—**Erick Peters**, Federal Healthcare Chief Technology Officer

"*Disrupted* offers a practical, confidence-building approach that empowers individuals and teams to navigate failure, overcome adversity, and create meaningful, transformational change."
—**Mashea M. Ashton**, Founder and CEO, Digital Pioneers Academy

"Nuggets of wisdom shine as Thornton's brilliance enlightens us to be our best selves. Get ready to take action through real-world examples that will resonate with you. Thornton's insights will inspire you toward greater clarity in your life."
—**Toacca Rutherford**, Managing Director, JPMorganChase

"A fascinating and accessible explanation of human behavior and growth, examined through the lens of brain physiology as an engineered system."
—**Bryan Rychlik**, Senior Vice President, Simpson Strong-Tie Company

"Disruption isn't a detour. It's the road. Thornton's 2 Stabilizers and 7 Accelerators give leaders what matters most—agency in uncertainty. This is engineering rigor applied to human resilience. Disruption isn't what you survive—it's what you rise on."
—**Maurice "Moe" Spencer**, Senior Manager, Technical Services, Everpure (formerly Pure Storage)

DISRUPTED

DISRUPTED

THE 2 STABILIZERS AND 7 ACCELERATORS OF GROWTH THROUGH CHAOS

ANDRE W. THORNTON

Published by Learn-It-All Press
Sausalito, CA
www.learnitallpress.com
For permissions or bulk sales inquiries: info@learnitallpress.com

First Edition

Names: Thornton, Andre W., author.
Title: Disrupted : the 2 stabilizers and 7 accelerators of growth through chaos / by Andre W. Thornton.
Description: Includes bibliographical references. | San Francisco, CA: Learn-It-All Press, 2026.
Identifiers: LCCN: 2026902037 | ISBN: 979-8-9941708-4-7 (paperback) | 979-8-9941708-5-4 (ebook)
Subjects: LCSH Leadership. | Corporate culture. | Success in business. | Success. | Self-actualization (Psychology). | Self-help. | BISAC BUSINESS & ECONOMICS / Leadership | BUSINESS & ECONOMICS / Workplace Culture | SELF-HELP / Personal Growth / Success
Classification: LCC HF5386 .T46 2026 | DDC 650.1--dc23

Design by Molly Sokolow Hayden

Printed in the USA
10 9 8 7 6 5 4 3 2 1

This book provides general information on leadership and business management. It is sold with the understanding that the publisher and author are not engaged in rendering legal, accounting, medical, or other professional services. While every effort has been made to ensure accuracy, the work is provided "as is," without warranties, and neither the author nor the publisher shall be liable for any loss or damages arising from its use.

To Jo Jo

TABLE OF CONTENTS

INTRODUCTION

In October 2013, I was staring down what felt like the collapse of everything I had worked for. Just the year before, I had embarked on a life-changing journey to Africa and, soon after, uprooted my life, moving from Georgia to Maryland to step into an executive role at Lockheed Martin. After sixteen relentless years of climbing the engineering ranks to the director level, my career was reaching a new high—or so I thought. But then came the news: The company was slashing leadership positions, cutting the number of directors from forty-four to just nineteen. We were all required to reapply for the roles we had built our careers around. I did and found myself out of a job.

For an engineer trained to optimize systems and solve complex technical problems, the loss of this role felt like a fundamental failure. But engineers are stubborn people, so what emerged from the crisis wasn't just a career pivot; it was a complete reimagining of how leadership works. This book is the product of that journey through disruption, using the systematic approach to personal and leadership development that emerged from my personal experience and research.

Disruption has a strange way of clearing the noise. It revealed something I'd always known but never fully admitted: I cared more about people than planes. I wasn't just an engineer—I was a people engineer. And that realization set me off in a different direction. Within Lockheed Martin, I moved into a leadership development role and began applying my engineer's mindset to the challenges of human growth and organizational transformation.

Throughout my youth and professional life up to that point in 2013, I had believed that I would eventually "arrive"—and on that day, I'd have it all figured out. When we're children, it's easy to look at adults and think they're all grown up. We think we'll grow up too, imagining "grown up" as a destination where we'll become the person we've always wanted to be. We picture finally stopping the painful growing and becoming phase to just be. We hurry through our early twenties in an urgent quest to be successful, be confident, be grown up. But I've come to believe that's a mistake.

We all inevitably get older. Many of us become responsible adults. But ideally, we never stop growing up.

I've found the real work of my maturity is to continually raise my baseline, shorten my recovery time, and turn each challenge into another catalyst of my perpetual growing up. This is what I mean when I say, "Fall down, grow up." Every challenge then naturally provides the gift of upward growth.

Along the way, I've had the privilege of helping thousands of leaders—from Fortune 500 executives to solo entrepreneurs—turn their own moments of upheaval into moments of growth. So if life feels chaotic right now and you're facing a frightening or overwhelming disruption, congratulations! You're in the best possible situation to keep on growing up.

TAKE A MOMENT
What kind of person would you be right now if you had never faced a situation that pushed you well beyond your comfort zone?

WHY THIS BOOK, AND WHY NOW?

Disruption is no longer an exception—it's the environment we live in. Whether it's global instability, economic uncertainty, organizational shake-ups, or deeply personal turmoil, life keeps reminding us that control is limited and certainty is fleeting. We're not living in a world of one-off setbacks; we're living through a systemic shift.

When you have a high degree of certainty in your life, things feel stable. But nature seems to treat stability the same way it does a vacuum. Change is inevitable, and with it, the loss of predictability. If that change is sudden, unexpected, or unwanted, and life- or identity-threatening, it pitches us into disruption. And often, when disruption hits—personal, professional, or external—our default is to tighten our grip. We double down on what has worked in the past. We avoid risk. We retreat into familiar patterns or overplan, hoping to outsmart the unknown.

This is how most people get trapped in what I call the Control-Certainty Paradox: The more you try to control uncertain situations, the more out of control you feel. The harder you grasp for certainty, the more slippery everything becomes.

ESCAPE THE MATRIX

To escape this paradox, we need to separate control from certainty and understand how conflating them keeps us stuck.

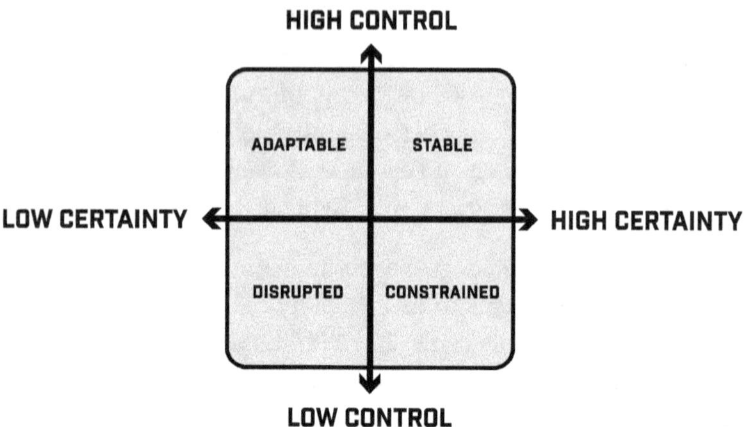

Constrained is where many people live by default. Things are predictable and familiar, but you have little power to change them. You know what to expect from your job, your relationships, and your routine, but you can't influence the outcomes. Often, this position feels safe, but it's not quite comfortable. It's the home of Thoreau's "lives of quiet desperation."

Stable is much more comfortable. You're in control of your life. Your systems work, your processes are optimized, and you can predict outcomes with reasonable accuracy. Everything runs smoothly (if not joyfully)—until disruption hits and reveals how fragile your "control" really was.

Disrupted is where most people land when the unexpected strikes. In disruption, both control and certainty disappear. It's painful and frightening. Under these circumstances, we tend to freeze or fall apart, the amygdala hijacks rational thinking, and we suffer.

Adaptable is where growth happens. You don't know how things will play out, but you do know that you've developed enough agency to respond, experiment, and adapt by taking control of what you can—yourself. You can't predict the outcome, but you *can* influence the process.

For leaders—especially those trained to optimize, predict, and control every variable—times of disruption can feel especially destabilizing. Our instincts push us toward precision, planning, and the prioritization of security. But leading ourselves and others through disruptive times demands something different: We must shift from being engineers of systems to engineers of resilience. We cannot stabilize the world. The ground is going to keep moving under our feet. We can only increase our agility. We can stop racing toward ever-changing destinations and instead focus on raising the quality of the journey. We can turn the trudge into a dance.

This book is your partner in making that shift. It's not a prescriptive system but rather a dynamic set of core moves and principles you can adapt to suit your unique journey. To move from disruption into the productive space of adaptability, you first need tools to help you recover quickly from each setback and grow up a little more each time you fall (Part 1: Find Your Footing). You then need practical ways to quickly turn setbacks into momentum, clarify your purpose, and engineer your strengths (Part 2: Move with Purpose). Finally, you need a way to ramp up the trust, alignment, and ownership of your teams so that you and they can grow—and keep growing—forward together (Part 3: Lift Others as You Rise).

DISRUPTION IS INEVITABLE, BUT WITH THE RIGHT STABILIZERS AND ACCELERATORS, IT CAN BECOME THE ENGINE OF GROWTH.

FROM AEROSPACE TO HUMAN SYSTEMS

Everything I teach in this book is rooted in a mindset I carried over from my engineering days: the belief that complex systems can be understood, improved, and optimized—if you use the right frameworks and adapt them to the realities of human life.

What makes this work different is that instead of designing fighter jets, we're designing lives, careers, and teams that can thrive in unpredictable environments. I still think like an engineer, but now, I apply that thinking to people. Processes matter. But in human systems, emotion, motivation, and identity matter even more.

This book brings those two worlds together: the structured rigor of engineering and the messy brilliance of human growth.

WHO THIS BOOK IS FOR

This book is for people in transition—whether you chose the change or the change chose you. It's for the engineer who just got promoted and realizes leading people requires a different tool kit. It's for the seasoned leader navigating burnout, the founder pivoting after a market shake-up, and the professional wondering what's next after a layoff or life event. Whether you're in the C-suite or the coffee shop, this book will help you turn each disruption into a catalyst for growth and every fall into a challenge to grow up stronger.

HOW THIS BOOK IS STRUCTURED

Disrupted is built around a simple but powerful progression designed to help you harness disruption as fuel for growth. It begins with two stabilizers—practices that ground you in clarity and resilience so that you can stay steady when circumstances shift. From there, it introduces three self-leadership accelerators that drive internal transformation, helping you develop the mindset, habits, and emotional agility to turn uncertainty into forward motion. Finally, it loops in four additional accelerators focused on leading others, equipping you to guide teams and organizations through change by converting it into shared momentum and sustained success.

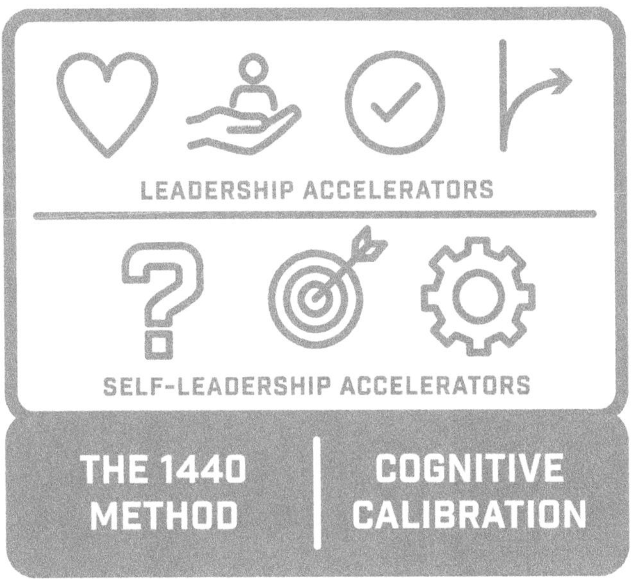

READING + REPS

In Parts 2 and 3, each chapter concludes with a set of small, targeted actions you can take immediately. You don't build muscle by reading about weightlifting, and the same is true of mental fitness. These aren't elaborate projects or time-consuming assignments. They're the equivalent of a single set at the gym, because in my experience, a tiny action you'll complete beats a grand plan you'll perpetually postpone. Repeat them consistently, and you'll gradually rewire your brain to be stronger, more resilient, and able to handle ever greater challenges.

Disruption might knock the wind out of you. But it can also push you toward a version of yourself you didn't know was possible. If you're ready to stop waiting for things to go back to normal and start building something better, one "fall down, grow up" moment at a time, I wrote this book for you.

Let's begin.

PART 1

FIND YOUR FOOTING

CHAPTER 1

WHAT HAPPENS WHEN THE WORLD BREAKS YOUR PLANS

As a Lockheed Martin executive overseeing two thousand people and having received sixteen years of steady promotions, I thought my job was bulletproof. With a long-standing habit of treating every career decision like a systems engineering problem, I'd done everything career advice books and mentors had told me to do. I'd built resilience through planning, backup strategies, and risk mitigation. I was an engineer, after all; I had contingency plans for my contingency plans. None of it mattered when I found myself interviewing for a job I'd thought I owned and didn't make the cut.

At the same time, my marriage was struggling. In the span of a few months, I went from thinking I had everything under control to sitting in my home office, staring at the wall, wondering what had just happened. You know that moment when you're driving a familiar road, so confident in the route that you stop paying attention and miss a critical turn? That was me. I had been cruising on autopilot, and the road vanished.

DISRUPTION NEVER ASKS, "IS NOW A GOOD TIME?"

Instead of wallowing (okay, I wallowed a little), I did something that surprised even me. I finally stopped fighting what I'd always known about myself and started taking my lifelong interest in mentoring and leadership seriously. All those years, I'd been dismissing my interest in personal development as, well, *personal*. But in the midst of all that disruption, I began to wonder if what I was experiencing was less of an ending and more of a redirection. I started building frameworks for how people grow. I got obsessed with understanding transformation—how individuals and teams change, not despite disruption but because of it. I turned that crisis into a catalyst, then into a curriculum.

By 2016, I was ready to make an even more terrifying leap. After two years of working in leadership development at Lockheed Martin, I walked away from the steady paycheck and health insurance to start my own leadership development company. Whitman Consulting was born two weeks after my son, Carter. My wife still jokes that she was too distracted being pregnant to properly panic about my leaving a stable corporate job to chase what probably looked like a crazy dream.

Today, Whitman Consulting has been recognized as one of the top ten leadership development firms, and I'm doing the work I'm meant to be doing in this phase of my life—helping people build their stabilization stack and raise their baseline so that they can lead first themselves and then others through uncertainty. If I hadn't been disrupted, I'd probably still be sitting in that corporate office, technically successful but quietly miserable, wondering why a perfectly good career felt like wearing someone else's clothes. The path between being laid off and hanging out my shingle wasn't easy, but it taught me something crucial: Disruption isn't a detour. It's the road.

THE MYTH OF THE BACKUP PLAN

We're taught that preparation is the antidote to uncertainty and that we should equip ourselves with shock absorbers like emergency funds and a diversified skill set. This well-intentioned advice isn't wrong, but it's incomplete. It assumes disruption is an exception that we can insulate ourselves against.

The data suggests otherwise. In the fifty years between 1965 and 2015, there was a fourfold increase in the per-year failure rate of publicly traded companies.[1] And the World Economic Forum reports that 44 percent of workers' core skills are expected to change within the next five years.[2] This isn't episodic disruption, it's epochal.

Yet most of us still operate on twentieth-century assumptions. We build five-year plans in a world where the average S&P 500 company lasts eighteen. We save for linear retirements in nonlinear markets. We teach our kids to follow paths that might not exist when they graduate, rather than to prepare for roles we can't even imagine—although over 20 percent of professionals hired in the US today have job titles that didn't exist in 2000.

We're not just overconfident in the accuracy of our forecasts; we're overconfident in the idea that forecasting can be accurate. Our response mechanisms are built for a stable world. We're wired to believe tomorrow will look like today. That's what makes disruption feel not just disorienting but overwhelming.

---

1   Madeleine Daepp et al., "The Mortality of Companies," *Journal of the Royal Society, Interface* 12, no. 106 (May 2015), https://doi.org/10.1098/rsif.2015.0120.

2   World Economic Forum, "The Future of Jobs Report 2023," April 30, 2023, https://www.weforum.org/reports/the-future-of-jobs-report-2023.

THE NEUROSCIENCE OF DISRUPTION

Neuroscientist Lisa Feldman Barrett's research shows that our
brains are essentially prediction machines, constantly creating
models of what will happen next based on our past experiences.[3]
Disruption doesn't just break your plans—it breaks your prediction engine. It shakes your faith in your ability to interpret and
navigate the world. It doesn't just challenge what you know; it
challenges who you are. When you lose a job, a role, or a relationship that defined you, your very sense of identity dissolves. The
sentence "I am a…" trails off.

That's what happened to me. Andre W. Thornton, Lockheed Martin
engineer, died when I lost that job. And yes, it hurt. But it also
made space for Andre W. Thornton, people engineer, to emerge.

When disruption dismantles our predictive models, it triggers a
rare neurocognitive opening in which the brain's capacity to reconfigure its own circuitry becomes especially active. This process,
termed "neuroplasticity" by neurophysiologist Jerzy Konorski,
allows us to adapt to new circumstances by repatterning how we

---

3   Lisa Feldman Barrett, *How Emotions Are Made: The Secret Life of the Brain*
(Houghton Mifflin Harcourt, 2017).

think.[4] The same instability that makes disruption disorienting also makes it catalytic, allowing us to revise our natural intuitions in light of new, counterintuitive truths. Each of the growth accelerators we'll explore in Parts 2 and 3 leverages this disruption-induced neuroplasticity to speed and enable growth by replacing old, limiting ideas with more expansive and adaptive ones.

ENGINEERING PEOPLE

In the void left by my job loss, I started to pay more attention to something about myself that I'd been dismissing for years. Even as an aerospace engineer building sophisticated aircraft, I had always been more interested in the people than the planes. I'd spend lunch breaks mentoring junior engineers, volunteer for cross-functional team projects, and find myself in conversations about career development rather than technical specifications.

I'd been treating this interest as a distraction from my "real" work. But sitting in my home office staring at sixteen years of performance reviews that praised my "people skills" alongside my technical competence, I realized I'd been fighting my own wiring.

I began to think about my identity in a different way. What if I approached human development in the same way I approached engineering problems, with systems thinking, measurable inputs and outputs, and iterative improvement? What if personal resilience wasn't about emotional toughness but about engineering a better mechanism for turning chaos into growth? Those questions became the foundation of my work.

---

4   Jerzy Konorski introduced the concept of neuroplasticity (then neuronal plasticity) in his book *Conditioned Reflexes and Neuron Organization* (Pergamon Press, 1948).

2 STABILIZERS AND 7 ACCELERATORS FOR A DISRUPTED WORLD

Over the several years that followed, I developed this approach, initially testing it on myself and then with clients—including Fortune 500 executives and rising leaders navigating a wide range of challenges, from layoffs to IPOs. Three tools emerged, not as life hacks but as a new mental architecture for uncertain times:

STABILIZER 1: THE 1440 METHOD

This is a time discipline system based on the reality that we all get exactly 1,440 minutes each day. It's not time management; it's attention architecture. Most people leak energy to activities that seem urgent but create no momentum. The 1440 Method helps build what I call "directional time" minutes that compound toward something meaningful, even if you don't know exactly what that is.

STABILIZER 2: COGNITIVE CALIBRATION

I recommend a neuroscience-backed approach to regulating your brain chemistry in real time, consisting of approaches called DOSE and the Triple R Framework. When negative emotions hijack your prefrontal cortex, these micro-interventions act as tuning dials, restoring access to your higher-order thinking. The compound effect isn't just feeling better in the moment; it's making consistently better decisions that accumulate into measurable improvements in performance and quality of life.

THE 7 ACCELERATORS

This leadership development framework offers more than a sequence of steps—it transforms the destructive energy of chaos into a catalyst for growth:

1. Embrace uncertainty.
2. Put "why" over "what."
3. Engineer your strengths.
4. Be vulnerable.
5. Care about others.
6. Inspire accountability.
7. Want to be wrong.

Most people try to minimize disruption or simply endure it. These two stabilizers and seven accelerators do the opposite: They capture that volatile energy and redirect it toward accelerated development. The two stabilizers help you engineer your own resilience. The first three accelerators focus on self-leadership, while the remaining four scale that leadership outward, empowering you to lead teams and organizations through uncertainty—not by eliminating chaos but by converting it into momentum. Rather than progress being derailed by disruption, it's catalyzed by it.

These are the tools that helped me rebuild. They've since helped others do the same. You'll learn more about the two stabilizers in the following chapters. The seven accelerators of our leadership system are the focus of Parts 2 and 3.

WHEN THINGS FALL APART

Stanford economist Paul Romer called a crisis "a terrible thing to waste," and the data supports him. A 2020 McKinsey study found that companies that actively invested in transformation (particularly innovation) through the 2009 financial crisis ended up outperforming the market average by more than 30 percent and maintained their advantage over the next three to five years.[5]

The same holds true for individuals. It's not the grittiest or the best prepared who thrive but those who learn to use disruption as a signal, a clarifier, and a catalyst—because, despite how it may feel, disruption is a gift. It forces us to stretch in ways we never would have chosen on our own. It builds muscles we didn't know we had.

If, rather than resisting disruption or treating it as an obstacle, you can start to reframe it as more of an opening, you'll tap into the most creative and productive parts of your brain—the parts that see patterns where others see chaos. You'll find connections across seemingly unrelated domains and generate novel solutions precisely because conventional approaches no longer suffice.

That's what this book is about.

Whether you're navigating a personal loss, a career pivot, or an industry-wide shake-up, the message is the same: You don't need a clear path to make progress; you need the tools to navigate the pathless places. Armed with those tools, you only need to know the first step.

---

5   Jordan Bar Am et al., "Innovation in a Crisis: Why It Is More Critical than Ever," McKinsey & Company, June 17, 2020, http://www.mckinsey.com/capabilities/strategy-and-corporate-finance/our-insights/innovation-in-a-crisis-why-it-is-more-critical-than-ever.

CHAPTER 2

LEAD YOURSELF FIRST

I wasn't supposed to be the guy making the game-saving play. I was the quiet, skinny kid from Richmond, Virginia, who didn't really stand out much, definitely not for being the most athletic, confident, or bold. I'd started playing football because I liked the structure and the challenge. And let's be honest: The pads made me look a little tougher than I was.

Somewhere along the way, I got pretty good. Good enough to land a college scholarship. Good enough to start. Good enough to find myself lined up one Saturday across from Terrell Owens. Yes, *that* Terrell Owens.

In that moment, staring down a future Hall of Famer, I didn't feel good. I felt vaguely sick, like the little kid I used to be—unsure, outmatched, and two seconds from letting fear decide what I would do next. The quarterback glanced my way. I knew the ball was coming to me. My brain suggested the locker room was a nice, safe place.

But something in me didn't listen.

We were approaching the end zone. I planted my foot, jumped the route, and stretched out midair—full extension, hands out, heart pounding. Time slowed. I got just enough of the ball to tip it, and it wobbled to the ground like a wounded duck. The crowd exploded, my teammates swarmed me, and I just stood there for a second, stunned. Because I'd done it. I'd made *the* play. Against Terrell freaking Owens.

That one leap of faith, instinct, and self-trust changed how I thought about myself—not just as a player, but as a person. It was the first time I understood what it meant to lead myself: I didn't have it all figured out, but I chose to act despite the doubt. That's what self-ownership is. It doesn't mean you always know what you're doing. It means you take the leap anyway.

YOU CAN'T LEAD OTHERS UNTIL YOU CAN LEAD YOURSELF

That's not a slogan. It's an operating truth. You can't guide a team through pressure if you fold under it. You can't call others to clarity if your internal compass is spinning out of control. And you definitely can't build trust if your actions and values are out of alignment. Leadership, in its most sustainable form, doesn't begin with authority but with ownership.

BEFORE WE CAN STEADY OTHERS THROUGH DISRUPTION, WE MUST MASTER OUR OWN STABILITY.

WHAT SELF-LEADERSHIP MEANS

If you ask ten people to define leadership, you'll probably get ten versions of "inspiring others" or "achieving results." If you ask them to define *self*-leadership, you may just get a blank stare. It's all too easy to overlook the most obvious truth: The hardest person to lead is yourself.

Yet research shows we're not nearly as good at leading ourselves as we think. According to organizational psychologist Tasha Eurich, 95 percent of people believe they're self-aware, but in reality, only about 10 to 15 percent truly are.[6] That gap matters, because self-awareness isn't just a feel-good trait; it's a crucial aspect of personal growth and a key predictor of performance, influence, and leadership effectiveness. If we can't see ourselves clearly, we'll struggle to lead others with clarity and integrity.

This isn't theoretical for me. It took years of stumbling, trial and error, and what I call "soul audits" to realize that how I showed up when nobody was watching mattered more than how I performed when the spotlight was on me. Early in my leadership journey, I was always chasing tactics: frameworks, models, personality types. But I wasn't chasing clarity: *Who am I? What do I stand for? Where am I going, and what kind of person do I want to be on the way there?*

Those questions, asked consistently, form the foundation of self-leadership. When you can answer them honestly, your experience begins to shift. Your presence stabilizes. Your decision-making sharpens. And whether or not you have a title, people start to follow your lead.

**SELF-LEADERSHIP IS THE PRACTICE OF TAKING FULL
RESPONSIBILITY FOR HOW YOU SHOW UP, ESPECIALLY
WHEN THINGS ARE HARD, UNCLEAR, OR UNFAIR.
TO ACHIEVE IT, YOU NEED TO DEFINE YOUR VALUES,
BUILD SELF-TRUST, AND PRACTICE.**

---

6   Tasha Eurich, "What Self-Awareness Really Is (and How to Cultivate It)," *Harvard Business Review*, Jan. 4, 2018, https://hbr.org/2018/01/what-self-awareness-really-is-and-how-to-cultivate-it.

WHAT YOU STAND FOR

When disruption hits, it's easy to fixate on everything you've lost—structure, certainty, goals, momentum. But remember, you haven't lost your values. When everything else is up for debate, your values provide a guide to move forward, without needing every step to be mapped out in advance.

Even when the outcomes are unclear and the environment keeps shifting, you can choose to act in alignment with your values. That might mean generosity in the face of scarcity or honesty in a conversation where spin would be safer. Maybe it means choosing curiosity when frustration feels easier. When you don't know what comes next, your values give you something to stand on and for, a kind of internal certainty in an uncertain world. And sometimes, that's all you need to take the next step.

Moments of chaos are also moments of truth. They test your convictions. Some may not survive the test and need refinement, others keep you afloat, and still others will challenge you, asking you to prove your commitment to them. You may articulate your values in a mission statement, but you prove them through the trade-offs you make.

You prove your values when you decide not to chase the flashy opportunity that doesn't align with your long-term vision or when you walk away from a lucrative deal because it compromises your integrity. That's what I had to do when I turned down a six-figure contract that would've put my company in front of major players, because it came with strings I wasn't willing to ignore. Walking away wasn't easy, but it was aligned.

Self-leadership means being willing to pay the price of integrity, not just to say, "These are my values," but to absorb the cost of living them. Disruption often provides an ideal (if not convenient) opportunity to do so.

List three values you refuse to compromise, even under pressure. When was the last time they guided a hard decision?

ADAPTABILITY VS. AUTHENTICITY

Staying true to your values doesn't require you to be rigid. Self-leadership isn't about being inflexible, but it is about being anchored. Sometimes that means adapting how you show up. Sometimes it means adjusting your tone, language, or approach to fit the room. That's not inauthenticity. That's emotional intelligence.

The key is to avoid confusing adaptation with abandonment. You can flex without folding. You can meet people where they are without losing who you are. The test is whether the version of you that shows up in a new room is still operating from your values or from your fear.

When the path gets foggy, your values are your compass. Within each context, choose the most appropriate version of yourself that still embodies your values. This may be the most conforming version or the most controversial, but that's not the determining issue. As long as it's true, it's right.

In disruption, your values are your guide, but they're also a signal. They show others who you are and what's possible. They give your team something solid to believe in and calibrate against. And they give you a way to stay grounded when the world is trying to blow you off course.

WHERE SELF-LEADERSHIP BEGINS

Self-leadership begins with steadiness. Not certainty, not control—just the steady willingness to choose from your values, even when fear is louder. When the moment feels high-stakes or high-pressure, your clarity becomes your compass. It points you toward the kind of leader you want to be and gives you the footing to move in that direction, one decision at a time.

Private victories precede public victories.
—Stephen Covey

Leadership doesn't start when you're handed a mic or a mandate. It's the quiet, private choices, when no one's watching and the stakes feel small, that shape you. They train your instincts and reinforce your identity. Self-leadership takes root in the consistent alignment between what matters to you and how you move through the world.

Early in my consulting career, I realized I was talking about values more often than I was living them. That led me to do a soul audit. I had to ask myself: *Am I living what I say I value, or am I just performing a version of leadership that looks good on paper?*

That's not a comfortable question, but it's a necessary one. When your words and actions diverge, your team can feel it. More importantly, you feel it, and that disconnect erodes your credibility from the inside out.

Of course, leading from values doesn't guarantee every decision will be easy—or even "right." But it does guarantee that you'll be able to live with your decisions. And that's the kind of integrity that endures.

SELF-LEADERSHIP IS BUILT THROUGH PRACTICE

People often overcomplicate the development of self-leadership, thinking it requires a grand reinvention or total overhaul of their lives and work patterns. It doesn't. Self-leadership is less about fixing and more about noticing. *When am I triggered? When am I avoiding something? When am I pretending not to know what I actually do?* These moments aren't failures—they're invitations.

I often ask clients, "What does the best version of you look like—not on a stage or in a LinkedIn post, but on a regular Tuesday afternoon? And what's one small decision you could make today to move toward that version?"

That's the work. That's the muscle. Each time you act in a way that reflects your values, you reinforce them and prove to yourself that you can be trusted with your own future. Over time, that internal alignment gives you the capacity to hold space for others.

I spoke to the Washington Spirit leadership team right after Magic Johnson invested in the franchise. The stakes were high. Pressure was everywhere. And I told them what I'm telling you now: Before you lead the scoreboard, lead yourself.

That message landed. Even elite performers need the occasional reminder that performance starts with presence. Presence starts with intention. And intention starts with knowing who you are and making the choice to act accordingly.

THE SELF-LEADERSHIP LOOP

Self-leadership is a rhythm: awareness, alignment, accountability, adaptation—over and over. You don't graduate from it; you grow through it. I call it the 4-A Self-Leadership Loop. Every challenge becomes another turn through the loop, another rep that makes you stronger, clearer, and more resilient. It consists of four core moves:

1. AWARENESS

You can't lead what you won't look at. Self-leadership begins with paying attention, especially to the stuff you'd rather ignore. That flash of frustration in the meeting? The knot in your stomach before a hard conversation? The way you said yes when everything in you meant no? Those are signals, not flaws. Awareness involves noticing your patterns, triggers, and internal weather. It's pressing pause long enough to ask: *What's actually going on here?*

2. ALIGNMENT

Once you see clearly, the next step is to make a deliberate choice. Alignment begins in the moment your values start showing up in your actions. It's when your decisions carry your signature, not because they're perfect but because they reflect the person you're becoming. The more often you make those choices, the easier it is to recognize yourself in the results. It's saying, *This is what matters, so this is what I'm going to do*—even when it's inconvenient, unpopular, or scary.

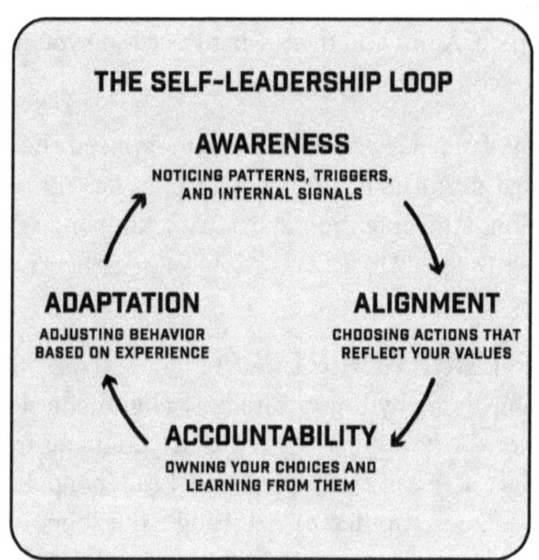

3. ACCOUNTABILITY

This is the part where most people flinch, but without accountability, it's just talk. Accountability means owning your choices—even when the results aren't what you hoped. It's asking: *Where did I wobble today? What story am I telling myself? What would it look like to show up more honestly tomorrow?* It's not about guilt—it's about growth.

4. ADAPTATION

Every cycle is a chance to adjust—to notice what worked, what didn't, and what needs to shift. Adaptation is where self-leadership becomes resilience. It's how you build agility without compromising your core. It's saying: *That version of me made the best decision they could with what they knew. Now I know more.*

And then? You loop back again. Awareness. Alignment. Accountability. Adaptation. It's not a checklist—it's a rhythm. A muscle. A way of leading yourself that holds steady even when the world around you doesn't.

TAKE A MOMENT

Which of the four A's (awareness, alignment, accountability, or adaptation) is strongest for you right now? Which needs the most attention?

SELF-LEADERSHIP IS THE FOUNDATION OF ALL LEADERSHIP

Every kind of leadership begins with self-leadership. It's the anchor that keeps you steady in uncertainty and the compass that helps you choose your next move with intention. When you lead yourself well, it changes how others respond to you.

Leading yourself begins with awareness and loops through alignment and accountability to adaptation and back to awareness. It's grounded in small, decisive moments when you choose to speak up, set a boundary, and act in alignment with your values, even when it's uncomfortable. These are the moments that build trust, not only with others but also with yourself.

The more you trust yourself, the more deliberate you can be with your most precious resource—and time, when used with intention, becomes a force multiplier for everything you want to create.

Self-leadership is the foundation for all other forms of leadership. It's not optional. It's not fluffy. And it's not just for executives. It's for anyone who wants to move through disruption with clarity, consistency, and courage.

CHAPTER 3

THE 1440 METHOD

I used to think I was good at managing my time. My calendar was full, my inbox was (mostly) under control, and I knew how to hustle. Like most professionals, I could fill a day with meetings, tasks, and to-dos that made me feel productive.

Then, when the Lockheed Martin reorg disrupted my professional life, I found myself busy but untethered. It wasn't that I didn't have things to do; I just wasn't sure what mattered. I was managing time but not directing it. Because I'm an engineer, I recognized this as a resource-allocation problem. I added up the number of minutes in a day (1,440) and listed all the activities I was engaged in. I prioritized those actions and assigned them chunks of time. I called this (in typical engineer fashion) the 1440 Method.

You can't lead yourself—or anyone else—if your minutes are leading you. The 1440 Method helps you reclaim control of your most finite resource: time. It requires taking complete ownership of your life and provides a practical system for aligning your daily actions with your deepest values. It looks like a productivity tool, but it's really a resilience engine.

YOU HAVE ENOUGH TIME

Most people live with a constant, low-level anxiety known as "time scarcity"—the sense that there's never enough time to do everything you need to, let alone all the side projects and interests you'd like to explore. Many of us treat time as something to manage, squeeze, or hack. But the real problem isn't how much time we have; it's how we use it.

WHAT'S IN SHORT SUPPLY ISN'T TIME, BUT INTENTION.

Most people spend about 20 percent of their time in the deliberate pursuit of a preplanned task. They spend the rest of their time reacting—answering emails, attending meetings, and fulfilling obligations. But if we want to turn disruption into growth, we need to shift that balance by moving from obligation to intentionality.

1,440 MINUTES

Every day gives us 1,440 minutes. That's it—no more, no less. You don't get rollover minutes from yesterday's discipline, and you can't borrow from tomorrow's intentions. Yet most of us treat time like we've got a secret inheritance coming—some hazy future where things will "finally calm down" and we'll get around to what matters.

I used to think time management was about getting more done. Lists, calendars, hacks, apps—I tried them all. But productivity isn't the same as purpose. I've had days when I checked every box and still felt like I was falling behind. I've also had days when I moved one meaningful thing forward and felt like a superhero. That's what the 1440 Method is about: reclaiming your time not just from distractions but from default mode, autopilot, and the illusion that urgency always outranks importance.

The 1440 Method rests on four pillars—none of them are new, but together, they build a framework for designing your time around what matters most. First, clarify your intention by identifying the areas of your life that are most important to you and the kind of experience you want to have in each. Next, set clear goals designed to move yourself closer to what you've intentionally chosen. Then, define what I call an "average perfect day" to establish what your normal runtime will look like, filled with inspired actions directed toward reaching goals designed to create your desired experiences in the most critical areas of your life. Finally, build the habits that will help you move through your average perfect day without needing to exert constant, high levels of willpower.

How you spend your days is how you spend your life.
—**Annie Dillard**

CLARIFY YOUR INTENTION

First, you've got to know what your "big rocks" are. These aren't your to-do list items. They're the core domains of your life—the handful of areas that, when strong, make everything else work better. I am a Christian by faith, so for me, this process started and has continued with prayer. What emerged as I prayed was that family, health, work, spiritual practice, and financial abundance energize me. For you, the priorities might look different. The key is honesty.

Choose the five areas of your life that are most important to you and will become the foundation on which you'll structure the life you want to create. These are the things in your life you cannot and will not do without.

To clarify your five foundations, ask yourself:

- *What really matters to me?* (Not what *should* matter, what *does* matter.)
- *What do I spend most of my time and money on?*
- *Who are the most important people in my life?*
- *What can I not live without?*

Once you've identified the five most crucial areas of your life, create a vision for each by asking yourself:

- *What kind of life do I want?* (Not just this week or this quarter, but in the long run.)
- *What kind of family life, married life, work life, social life, and spiritual life do I want?*
- *What does "flourishing" look like in each of my five foundational areas?*

When I first sat down to do this for myself, I realized two things. The first was that I had vague aspirations like "be healthy" and "have a good marriage," but I didn't have a clear picture in my mind of what success would look and feel like. The second was that I had not given myself permission to imagine beyond the practical into the possible. As a kid, I'd had big dreams, but years of societal conditioning had atrophied my ability to want what I wanted from a place of genuine passion and purpose rather than a sense of obligation or propriety.

Vision brings clarity, gives your goals context, and pulls you forward. When you can see what you really want, you start moving toward it almost without trying. Motivation becomes less of a grind and more of a gravitational force.

Creating a vision for each of your five foundations requires time and reflection. Don't expect a well-defined and clear vision overnight. Commit to taking the time to figure this out. Be creative.

     DISRUPTED

Consider ideas that you never thought possible. Focus on your wishes, not what others expect of you. Continually remind yourself that a life of fulfillment happens not by chance but by design.

First, ask yourself:

- *What would bring more joy and happiness into my life?*
- *Setting aside financial considerations for a moment, what do I want from my career?*
- *What qualities and skills would I like to develop?*
- *What do I want all my interpersonal relationships to be like?*
- *What do I want spiritually?*
- *What legacy would I like to leave behind?*

Next, ask yourself: *Do I believe I deserve the life I've described?*

Our brains are very efficient at proving our beliefs right. They gather only the evidence that supports our beliefs and ignore the rest, so choose to believe that you deserve these visions and can make them your reality.

THE LIFE WHEEL

This is one of the simplest and most revealing tools I've found for reconnecting people with what matters most to them and for identifying areas where they may have quietly drifted from their purpose.

Here's how it works: Draw a circle. (Yes, we're going old-school with this. You can do it digitally, but paper and pen make it feel more real.) Divide your circle into five slices, like a pizza or a pie chart. Each slice represents one of your five foundations: family, health, career, spirituality, finances—whatever you identified as your five core life domains.

Then, for each slice, rate your current level of satisfaction on a scale from zero to ten. A zero means "This part of my life is basically on fire, and not in a good way." A ten means "This is exactly how I want it to be." Color in each slice proportionally to how aligned with your vision you feel that area of your life is. It's important that you separate how aligned it is from how well you're performing. It's easy to get stuck in a job you're good at, even if it has nothing to do with your vision for your professional life.

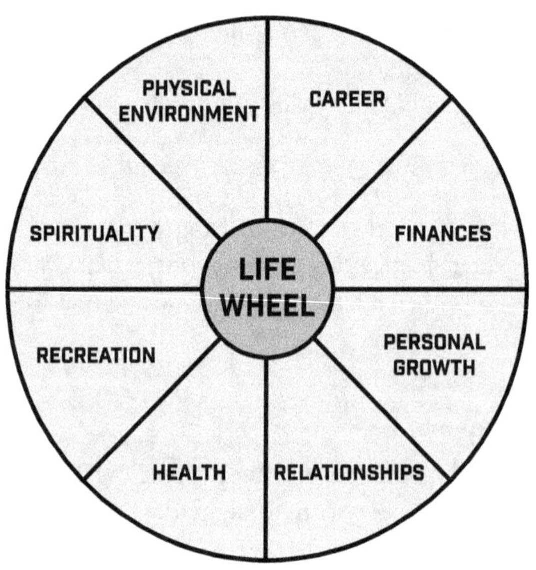

At first glance, this exercise may seem almost too simple, but I've found the impact can be startling. People look down at their completed Life Wheel and *immediately* see why they feel stuck or off-balance. Maybe your career is humming along at an eight, but your health is a two. Maybe your spiritual life has quietly dropped to a one, and you didn't even notice. Or perhaps you realize you've got some solid sixes across the board—but nothing lighting you up. No tens. No joy.

The point of the Life Wheel isn't to shame yourself or panic over the low numbers. It's simply to create awareness. When you visualize the shape of your life in this way—uneven, spiky, maybe a little deflated—it becomes easier to see where to focus your time and energy.

I always encourage people to complete their Life Wheel after they've articulated a vision for each area. That way, you're not just rating how you feel in the abstract; you're rating how close your current reality is to the life you want. That's what makes the exercise powerful. It's not just a mood check—it's a measure of alignment. Ultimately, the Life Wheel is less about scoring your life and more about owning it. It's a chance to pause—a quiet checkpoint in the chaos where you get to ask yourself, *Is this the life I meant to build?* And if the answer is no, you get to choose again.

Let the Life Wheel guide your priorities. Which area most needs your attention? Where would one meaningful change have the biggest ripple effect? That's where you set your next goals.

TAKE A MOMENT
Draw your own Life Wheel right now. Where are the biggest gaps?

CHOOSE GOALS THAT STRETCH YOU

Goals are how you build the bridge from your current self to your future self. The best ones should give you butterflies—not because they're unrealistic, but because you'll need to grow to reach them. The right kind of goal exists in that sweet spot between "I could do this in my sleep" and "There's no way." Crucially, these goals must connect to your vision. Otherwise, you'll end up climbing the ladder, only to find it's leaning against the wrong wall.

I used to think I didn't need goals. I was motivated. I had drive. I was already doing a lot. But I've come to realize that goals aren't just about outcomes; they're about awareness. When you get specific about what you're aiming for, you give yourself a daily feedback loop. If two weeks have passed and you're nowhere near halfway, that's not failure. That's clarity. It lets you recalibrate and recommit. And that clarity—especially during times of disruption—is everything.

The best goals live in the "growth zone," that sweet spot between comfort and panic. If a goal feels like something you could do in your sleep, it won't change you. If it feels completely impossible, it'll shut you down before you begin. But a stretch goal leads to transformation.

Here's a trick I use with clients: I ask them to imagine their eighty-year-old self—healthy, retired, at peace. Then I ask, "What would that version of you say should be your top priority right now?" That perspective almost always clears the noise. Your eighty-year-old self won't care about Instagram likes or inbox zero. They'll care about whether you showed up for what mattered: your health, your purpose, your people. Use your Life Wheel as your compass. What's calling for your attention? Where would progress create a ripple effect? Pick a goal that moves the needle, one your eighty-year-old self will be glad you chose. Then make it SMART.

SMART GOALS (WITH A TWIST)

You've probably heard of SMART goals: specific, measurable, actionable, relevant, time-bound. Let me give you an example. A weak goal sounds like "I'm going to get fit." A SMART goal sounds like "I'm going to follow the Nike Training Club app to complete a marathon without stopping six months from now."

See the difference? The second version provides you with a concrete goal to work toward and a clear deadline. It turns a foggy intention into a clear destination. It's a solid framework, but I want to add something crucial that most people miss: The best goals hit you in two places—your head and your heart. Your rational brain needs to see a logical path forward, even if you don't know every step yet. But your emotional brain needs to feel pulled toward the outcome. You do this by linking your goals to your intentions.

A GOAL THAT'S JUST RATIONAL IS A CHORE. A GOAL THAT'S JUST EMOTIONAL IS A WISH. BUT A GOAL THAT'S BOTH IS A CATALYST.

If your physical health is one of your Life Wheel sections (and it should be), but you scored yourself only a two in that area, you might start with the goal of getting fit. If your vision of flourishing is being strong, energetic, and capable of finishing a marathon, the SMART goal of doing so in six months with the help of the Nike Training Club app would be right on target.

Then, add "so that I…" to make it a SMARTI goal—specific, measurable, actionable, relevant, time-bound, *and inspiring* because it's rooted in a deeper intention. You're not just chasing a checkbox. You're chasing a vision of who you want to become.

SMARTI GOALS FRAMEWORK

S	M	A	R	T	I
SPECIFIC	MEASURABLE	ACTIONABLE	RELEVANT	TIME-BOUND	INSPIRING

Try It!

Take a look at your Life Wheel. Which area scored lowest? Which one, if improved, would make the most significant positive impact on the other areas of your life? Now, imagine your eighty-year-old self. What would they tell you to focus on in that area over the next year? What one significant change would they encourage you to make?

Make sure your goal passes these tests:

- It excites you—you feel energy when you think about achieving it.
- It scares you a little—you'll need to grow to reach it.
- It's specific enough that you'll know when you've achieved it.
- It connects to your deeper values and vision.
- It feels meaningful to your eighty-year-old self.

CHART THE AVERAGE PERFECT DAY

This is where the rubber meets the road—or, more accurately, where your calendar meets your character. Because ultimately, what fills your 1,440 minutes is what fills your life.

If your actions reflect your goals, your goals reflect your vision, and your vision reflects your foundation, you've gone beyond being productive to become *aligned*. You're not just doing things right; you're doing the right things.

Designing your day with intention doesn't require a color-coded calendar (though I've met people who swear by them). It just means asking yourself each morning: *What matters most today? What's one thing I can do that would make me proud when my head hits the pillow tonight?*

The 1440 Method challenges you to examine your average day: What are you doing? Who are you doing it with? Which actions feed your goals, and which feel like meaningless churn? Here, I'm talking about your daily actions—not your dreams or long-term plans, but the stuff that actually fills your Tuesday. The emails, the errands, the meetings, the workouts (or the skipped workouts), the snacks, the scrolls, the deep work, the distractions.

How many of those actions are both good for you *and* enjoyable?

If your answer is "very few," you're not alone. That's where the Inspired Action Grid comes in. It's a simple tool I developed to help people take a fresh look at how they spend their time and, more importantly, how they *feel* about how they spend their time.

THE INSPIRED ACTION GRID

Here's the basic idea. You map your daily actions across two axes:

- On the X-axis, plot how much you *enjoy* the activity (subjective, emotional, "Do I like this?").

- On the Y-axis, plot how *good* it is for you (objective, aligned with your goals or well-being).

This gives you four quadrants:

1. Low Joy / Low Value—These are your chitlins. (I'll explain.)
2. High Joy / Low Value—Think chocolate chip cookies.
3. Low Joy / High Value—Kale.
4. High Joy / High Value—Hello, salmon.

Chitlins and Chocolate Chip Cookies

Growing up, my dad used to serve chitlins on New Year's Day. The smell alone was enough to make me question my lineage. Everyone said, "Just try them with mustard." I did. Verdict: Worse than the smell. And not healthy. Eating chitlins is a bottom-left action: low joy, low value—things like doomscrolling or gossiping fall in this category for me. Let's call this quadrant what it is: a wasteland. Do less of the things that go in this square.

On the other hand, I *love* chocolate chip cookies. They bring me real joy, but not much nutritional value. Eating chocolate chip cookies is a bottom-right activity: high joy, low value. Things that go in this quadrant aren't evil; they're indulgences, but spending too much time here creates bloat. Moderation is the name of the game.

In the top left quadrant, we have things that are good for you but not much fun. Like kale. They're low-joy, high-value activities like working out when you don't feel like it or calling that incredibly gloomy and unpleasant family member. It's the right thing to do, but not something you enjoy. These things matter but don't always feel good. In this quadrant, there's a trick: Find ways to make these activities more enjoyable.

That brings us to the sweet spot in the top right: high joy, high value. For me, this is salmon. It's good for me and tastes fantastic. When you can shift more actions into this quadrant—either by changing *what* you do or *how* you do it—you start to experience something powerful: joy-fueled discipline, and that's where inspired action lives.

Inspired action isn't always easy, and it isn't always fun—but it *can* be both. The key is to find small ways to raise the enjoyment level of the things that already align with your values. For example, put that kale in a smoothie. You'll get all the nutritional benefits and none of the taste. Reframe obligations as privileges—you get to have a relationship with your family member. Looking for the *why* behind the *what* can turn "I have to" into "I get to."

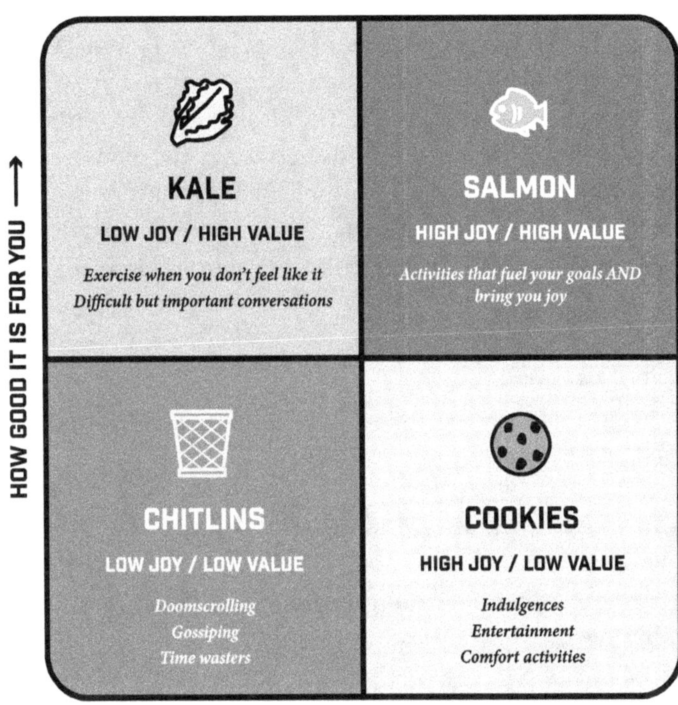

Try It!

Take a minute to jot down the elements of your typical day. What do you do? Who are you with? What's your mindset? Now ask:

- *Do I enjoy this?*

- *Is it good for me?*

- *Does it connect to any of my foundations?*

- *Does it move me toward my vision in any area of life?*

Then, plot each action on the grid.

You might find you're spending a surprising amount of time on things that don't support your goals, don't feel good, or both. That's okay. The goal here isn't guilt but awareness. Once you see where your time is going, you can begin to shift it—bit by bit—toward actions that are both nourishing and energizing. The more you fill your days with actions that are both aligned and alive, the more progress you make—and the better you feel while making it. That famous but elusive quest to "enjoy the journey" immediately becomes more accessible.

A DAY IN THE LIFE

Let me show you how this works by walking through a real day of mine. (Not a perfect day. Just a real one.)

6:00 a.m.—Wake Up and Meditate (High Joy / High Value)

I don't leap out of bed ready to greet the day like a motivational poster, but once I'm up, I head to the couch for ten minutes of quiet: deep breathing, centering, and sometimes prayer. It sets the tone for the day, and it's something I genuinely enjoy. Salmon.

6:30 a.m.—Work Out (High Value / Medium Joy)

I've had an evolving relationship with exercise over the years. It's changed from something I dreaded as a college athlete to something I enjoy as an adult. It's still hard to get going, but once I do, I feel good. Once I'm done, I feel great both physically and mentally. A home gym and simple workouts that I don't mind have certainly helped. Year by year, I'm slowly making exercise more like salmon.

7:45 a.m.—Get My Son Ready for School (High Value / Medium Joy)

This used to feel like a slog: the back-and-forth, the slow-motion toothbrushing routine before the rush out the door. But once I re-framed it as something I get to do (not have to do) with my kid, it shifted. Now, I try to make this time feel like connection, not just logistics. Still not salmon. Kale with a splash of joy.

9:00 a.m.—Email Triage (Low Joy / Medium Value)

Necessary? Sure. Fun? Not really. I set a timer and try to batch it. Otherwise, email expands to fill the void of real work. Classic kale—chew, keep chewing, swallow, move on.

9:30 a.m.—Client Coaching or Leadership Development Class (High Joy / High Value)

These are my favorite parts of the day. I get to see light bulbs go on. I get to help someone reconnect with who they are and what they want. This is peak inspired action: something I'm good at, something that matters, and something that lights me up.

12 noon—Scroll Instagram Reels for "Inspiration" (Low Joy / Low Value)

It starts as a break and ends with me watching a guy teach his cat to tap dance. This one lives in the chitlins quadrant. I don't truly feel great doing it (it's a false feel-good), and I don't feel great after. Awareness logged.

1:00 p.m.—Lunch and Walk (Medium Joy / High Value)

I used to eat at my desk. Now, I step away, eat mindfully, and take a quick walk—especially if the weather's good. Is it thrilling? No. But it clears my mind and supports my health. Quiet salmon.

2:00 p.m.—Content Writing (High Joy / High Value...Eventually)

This one depends on the day. Some days, I'm in flow. Other days, I'm wrestling with every sentence. But even on the hard days, it's work I believe in. When I set the right environment—music, snacks, no distractions—it moves solidly into inspired territory.

5:30 p.m.—Dinner and Family Time (High Joy / High Value)

This one is easy. It feeds my soul and my foundations. It doesn't have to be elaborate. Just being present with my family is salmon in its purest form.

9:00 p.m.—Netflix Wind-Down (Medium Joy / Low Value)

This is a slippery one. A good show can feel like a form of self-care. Bingeing three episodes of something I don't even like? Not so much. I try to keep it in balance—to treat it like cookies, not a food group. Watching TV with my wife, on the other hand, is all salmon all day.

When I step back and look at this kind of daily breakdown, a few things become clear:

- The more **top-right actions** I stack, the better my day feels.
- The more I reduce the **bottom-left** ones, the more energy I have.
- Even "necessary evils" can be redesigned by adding music, a friend, a change of scenery, or a smoothie.

The point of this exercise isn't to judge your actions but to understand them and then, bit by bit, to shift your days toward the actions that reflect your goals, your visions, and, ultimately, the life you want. After all, you only get 1,440 minutes today. Wouldn't it be great if more of them felt both meaningful and alive?

CREATE HABITS THAT CLOSE THE GAPS

By this point, you've clarified your intentions. You've set a compelling vision. You've defined SMARTI goals and charted an average perfect day. None of it will matter if you don't also develop habits that turn your goals, visions, and intentions into behaviors. This is where most of us stumble.

Research suggests that between a third and a half of our actions are habitual.[7] That's great news if your habits align with your goals. But most of us are trying to chase transformation with yesterday's wiring. If you're still operating from the same old mental model, with the same patterns, in the same comfort zone, you'll snap back to autopilot the moment disruption hits.

STRATEGY SETS THE GPS, BUT HABITS DRIVE THE CAR.

I played sports growing up, but after I left college and began my corporate life, I fell into a familiar pattern of starting strong but fading fast. With health as one of my five foundations, I created a vision of looking and feeling at least ten years younger than my age. To help me achieve that vision, I set a goal of exercising for at least thirty minutes four to five times per week and began taking the inspired action of working out in my basement on days when I could fit it in. But I wasn't being consistent with this action. I needed a habit.

Then, my daughter came home from her freshman year of college. She was struggling. Her grades were slipping, and she looked tired and defeated. I decided she needed structure—and not just any structure, but the kind that teaches you how to show up even when it's hard. I dusted off an old workout program and committed to doing it with her every morning at 6:30 a.m.

---

7   Wendy Wood et al., "Habits in Everyday Life: Thought, Emotion, and Action," *Journal of Personality and Social Psychology* 83, no. 6 (Dec. 2002): 1281–97, https://doi.org/10.1037//0022-3514.83.6.1281.

I am not a morning person.

I didn't want to work out at dawn. I didn't even want to be out of bed. But I wanted my daughter to succeed. So I built a system—one that made the new behavior obvious, attractive, easy, and satisfying. Sound familiar? They're James Clear's four laws of habit formation, and they work.

THE JAMES CLEAR ICEBERG

You can't power yourself to your goals by brute force—willpower and motivation wax and wane. Systems, on the other hand, make the right action the easiest one to take. Change the system, and behavior change will follow. Behavior change is like an iceberg. Systems are the portion below the waterline, and they're much larger and more consequential than the visible alteration they support.

Above the surface, you see events: Someone meets a deadline, a project launches, or a team hits a target. But beneath the surface are the patterns, structures, and mental models that produce those results—or sabotage them. So if you're struggling to take consistent action, don't start by beating yourself up. Start by redesigning the system. Stack the deck in your favor from below the waterline:

- **Make it obvious.** Set visual or time-based cues. Don't rely on memory—rely on design.

- **Make it attractive.** Tie the habit to something or someone you care about. Accountability amplifies follow-through.

- **Make it easy.** Shrink the action. Want to build a writing habit? Start with five minutes. Want to meditate? Sit in silence for thirty seconds. Lower the friction.

- **Make it satisfying.** Track it. Celebrate it. Reward it. Completion is a reward, but so is acknowledgment.[8]

The system I built to help my daughter (and me) form the habit of morning exercise was based on this iceberg method of behavior change. Rather than trying to white-knuckle it, I used all four subsurface laws to create momentum and lower the effort barrier.

- **Obvious:** We worked out at the same time every morning—no mental negotiation, no flexibility. It was on the calendar and in our routine.

- **Attractive:** I made myself accountable by doing it with her. I didn't just tell her to do it. I showed up for both of us.

- **Easy:** We used our home gym—no commute, no excuses.

- **Satisfying:** We put an "X" on a calendar each day we completed the workout. That simple ritual made progress visible and rewarding.

It didn't feel transformational at the time. Some mornings felt like punishment. But something shifted. I started working out more consistently than ever before. My daughter went back to school and pulled a 3.8 GPA. I'm not taking credit for her outstanding grades. I'm not even crediting the workouts. But I do think the accountability, structure, and ownership she developed that summer built more than muscles. They strengthened her mindset. (She even said so herself!) I continued the new habit on my own and, when I purchased a new Hume scale, it measured me as metabolically eleven years younger than my actual age. Vision achieved!

---

8   The iceberg concept and these principles are adapted from James Clear's *Atomic Habits* (Avery, 2018).

Habits aren't just what you do—they're who you're becoming. Each action you take is a vote for the kind of person you want to be. That's why the goal isn't just consistency but identity. When the habit stops being "something I do" and becomes "who I am," you've made the shift.

Transformation doesn't happen when you check every box. It happens when you design your day so that checking the box becomes second nature. That's why, at the end of my workshops, I put people into mastermind groups. The single most powerful reinforcement system is community. You want your new habit to stick? Don't do it alone. Find people who are trying to level up in the same way. Share your goals. Track your actions. Meet regularly. Celebrate progress. Accountability isn't pressure—it's permission to raise the water under everyone's boat.

DISRUPTION AND TIME

Disruption has a strange relationship with time. It can make the hours feel like sand slipping through your fingers. What once felt structured becomes slippery. Deadlines dissolve, priorities blur, and suddenly you're not sure if you've lost control of your time—or if time has somehow lost track of you. But it can also be a wake-up call to spend your minutes like they matter—because they do.

Disruption also has a way of stripping away illusion. It unmasks the autopilot routines, the false urgencies, the meetings we attended out of habit, and the habits we kept out of inertia. It forces us to confront how much of our lives are filled with noise. In the space where the old structure collapses, you get a choice: to rebuild with intention, or to stay tangled in the wreckage.

DISRUPTION DOESN'T STEAL TIME. IT REVEALS IT.

If you're in a season of change, make the most of it. Let it be your time audit. Pull back the curtain and ask: *Where is my time actually going? What am I doing because it aligns with who I want to become, and what am I doing just to survive the day?*

Even the simple act of tracking your time can be a grounding experience. It brings visibility to the invisible. When everything feels unstable, regaining time-awarencss is one of the most powerful stabilizers you have. Once you can see your minutes, you can start spending them like they matter.

HOW TO MANAGE YOUR MOST FINITE RESOURCE

You get 1,440 minutes each day. That's your whole inventory. You don't need to squeeze more in. You just need to stop giving so many away to things that don't serve you.

Disruption shakes us, but it also sharpens us. It's a reminder that our time is precious—and that clarity, discipline, and inspired action aren't luxuries. They're how we lead ourselves back to solid ground.

So if the ground beneath you is shifting, take a breath. Then take stock. Disruption may have changed your circumstances. But how you spend your minutes? That's still yours to choose.

CHAPTER 4

COGNITIVE CALIBRATION

I have a friend we'll call Don, to protect the not-so-innocent. Don is the poster child for what happens when you don't manage your internal chemistry. He's a successful guy, a great dad and father, and for 363 days of the year, a buttoned-up professional. He's the kind of person who color-codes his calendar and never misses a deadline. But every year, on the first night of our annual guys' trip, he absolutely loses his mind.

This isn't about the alcohol. It's about a year's worth of bottled-up stress, unprocessed emotions, and a desperate neurochemical need for connection and release. By the time we get together, Don has been running on cortisol and adrenaline for months, grinding through disruptions large and small—job pressures, family demands, financial stress—without ever giving his brain chemistry a chance to reset. He brings a year's worth of pent-up need to take the pressure off, let his guard down, and feel like he belongs without having to perform. Neurochemically, he's been running on empty, giving himself no room to breathe, let alone play. These weekends are his only release valve, and when it opens, everything flows out like wine. Or tequila.

Ironically, these trips are absolutely dripping with oxytocin—that feeling of having each other's backs, of belonging, of being part of something bigger than ourselves. It's the whole reason we go.

(Of course, we'd never say that out loud, because guys don't talk about that stuff. We just show up and pretend it's about golf.) And it's precisely what Don needs. It's only because he's waited until he's neurochemically depleted to seek it out that things can get out of control.

Don is a textbook example of what happens when we don't understand how to adjust our neurochemistry intentionally. Life disrupts our neurochemistry whether we're paying attention or not—through professional, personal, and financial challenges—and suddenly, we're operating from a place of fear and scarcity instead of abundance and possibility.

Disruption hijacks your brain chemistry, putting you in survival mode. But with small, intentional actions, you can trigger positive neurochemicals and shift into a more creative, focused, resilient state in the face of change. You can become disruption-ready, able to regulate your thoughts and feelings enough to stay calm, think creatively, and take meaningful action.

UPGRADE YOUR NEUROCHEMISTRY

When you're stressed, anxious, or triggered by unexpected change, your brain's wiring undergoes a dramatic shift. Blood flow moves away from the prefrontal cortex—the area responsible for logic, creativity, and long-term planning—and floods the limbic system, your brain's emotional command center. Psychologist Daniel Goleman coined the term "neural hijacking" to describe these moments when our emotional brain overrides our rational brain, in the neurological equivalent of trying to solve complex problems during a fire drill.[9]

---

9   Daniel Goleman, *Emotional Intelligence: Why It Can Matter More Than IQ* (Bantam Books, 1995), 25.

In these moments, your brain isn't prioritizing insight or innovation. It's prioritizing safety. It scans for threats. It narrows your thinking. It favors short-term, black-and-white decisions. From an evolutionary perspective, this makes sense. If a tiger is chasing you, you don't need to brainstorm five-year strategic plans; you need to run. But in modern life, that same system can be triggered by a tense meeting, an angry email, or a financial setback, and when we try to solve complex problems from this reactive state, we get tunnel vision, brittle thinking, and half-baked decisions.

Your internal chemistry shapes your external reality: How you feel shapes what you see, and what you see influences what you do. If your brain is bathed in stress hormones, even neutral situations can feel threatening, feedback can feel like an attack, and challenges can look like dead ends.

If you want better outcomes in your relationships, performance, and leadership, you need to operate from your best mental state, not your most reactive one. When your chemistry shifts, so does your perspective. You start to see options instead of obstacles and possibilities instead of problems. By deliberately dosing yourself with four feel-good chemicals your brain naturally produces (dopamine, oxytocin, serotonin, and endorphins, forming the acronym DOSE), you can quite literally dose your brain into better, more productive feelings, thoughts, and actions.[10]

YOUR INTERNAL PHARMACY

Your brain comes equipped with its own stash of "feel-good" chemicals that play a central role in how you think, feel, connect, and

---

10   TJ Power, *The DOSE Effect: Optimize Your Brain and Body by Boosting Your Dopamine, Oxytocin, Serotonin, and Endorphins* (Dey Street Books, 2025).

lead. These chemicals didn't evolve to make us happy but to help us survive. Long before emails and performance reviews, dopamine drove our ancestors to hunt for food and track patterns in the natural world. Oxytocin bonded us into tribes, where cooperation meant protection. Serotonin helped us navigate status and social structure, which influenced access to resources. And endorphins kicked in when we were wounded or exhausted, masking pain so that we could keep fighting or running away. They're biological tools you already use every day, whether you realize it or not. The key is learning how to activate them intentionally, especially in moments of disruption.

DOPAMINE, THE DRIVE TO STRIVE

Dopamine fuels forward motion and motivation. Counter-intuitively, it's not released when you achieve something but when you make progress toward it. You get a hit of dopamine when you set a goal or anticipate a treat. That little surge of "I'm getting close" is what keeps you going. It's nature's way of incentivizing effort. Unfortunately, modern life hands out cheap dopamine everywhere in the (too often successful) attempt to addict us to fast food, video games, and social media.

Intentionally satisfying your need for dopamine in a productive way means designing your day to include small wins, such as checking something off your list, completing a workout, or learning something new. Small rewards along the way to larger anticipated wins create momentum rather than addiction.

OXYTOCIN, THE COZY CHEMICAL

Oxytocin is often referred to as the "cuddle hormone," and for good reason. It's the neurobiological basis of trust, safety, and belonging. It gets released when we connect meaningfully with others through eye contact, shared purpose, or a genuine conversation. In tribal times, oxytocin told your nervous system, "You're not alone." In modern life, it still does. When you're going through disruption, oxytocin is a crucial stabilizer. Shame can make you want to keep your struggles to yourself, but one of the most powerful ways to restore resilience is to reach out and connect. A brief heart-to-heart, a hug, or even petting a dog can settle your neurochemistry in minutes.

SEROTONIN, THE CONFIDENCE OF CONTROL

Serotonin is released when we feel respected, secure, and in control of our lives. In contrast to oxytocin, which tends to derive from meaningful one-on-one interactions, and dopamine, which fires during pursuit, serotonin shows up when you look around and feel good about where you are. Serotonin is why recognition and rituals are both so deeply satisfying. Morning routines and weekly check-ins can increase serotonin levels, as can praise or thanks.

Disruption tends to strip us of control, and the consequent drop in serotonin levels is one of the reasons it's so unsettling. But we're not totally dependent on others to raise our serotonin. We can do it ourselves with consistency, self-respect, and values-based behavior.

ENDORPHINS, THE REAL RELIEF

Endorphins are your body's natural painkillers and stress relievers. They're released when you laugh, exercise, cry, or even eat spicy food. While dopamine gets you moving and oxytocin keeps you bonded, endorphins are how you exhale and recuperate. They create that lovely sensation of release and recovery, which is essential when you're navigating chaos. If you grind nonstop without endorphin breaks, you're running a pressure cooker without a vent. It's no accident that some of your clearest thinking happens after a run, a good laugh, or a cathartic movie.

YOUR INTERNAL PHARMACY

DOPAMINE	OXYTOCIN	SEROTONIN	ENDORPHINS
EFFECTS	**EFFECTS**	**EFFECTS**	**EFFECTS**
MOTIVATION AND REWARD	BONDING AND TRUST	MOOD AND WELL-BEING	PAIN RELIEF AND PLEASURE
TRIGGERS	**TRIGGERS**	**TRIGGERS**	**TRIGGERS**
•SETTING GOALS •MAKING PROGRESS	•PHYSICAL TOUCH •SOCIAL CONNECTIONS	•RECOGNITION •SENSE OF CONTROL	•EXERCISE •LAUGHTER

Because they feel good, your brain will always seek these chemicals; the only question is how. Scrolling gives you dopamine. Arguing on Twitter gives you a warped kind of serotonin. Instagram gives you quasi-oxytocin. But these are junk-food versions, quick hits that spike, crash, and leave you feeling worse.

Intentional dosing involves creating experiences that release these chemicals in sustainable ways. It's not about detoxing or perfection. It's about replacing the binge with the baseline. But understanding your neurochemistry is just the beginning. The real magic happens when you pair your ability to adjust your biology with ways of interrupting the thought-feeling-action loop that can keep you stuck.

TAKE A MOMENT

Which of the four chemicals are you naturally strongest at generating in your daily life? Which one do you most neglect?

THE C-WORD AND THE LOOP THAT LOCKS YOU IN

Cortisol is an anti-DOSE neurochemical that spikes anytime our brains detect a threat, and it's at the root of most of the bad feelings we have. Cortisol isn't "bad" in itself; it evolved to help us survive predators and danger. But in modern life, the same chemistry that once prepared us to fend off a panther can just as easily hijack a meeting.

When you see something, your brain interprets it, consciously or not. Most of these inputs are ignored, but some become thoughts that, in turn, spark a feeling that drives what you do next. Most of the time, this system works well. Your brain notices it's unusually dark as you're getting ready to leave for work. The observation turns into the thought *It might rain.* This triggers a slight release of cortisol, which you register as a feeling of mild concern, so you check the weather app on your phone. It tells you the day is likely to be cloudy and overcast but not rainy. This information drives a feeling of reassurance, since clouds likely won't impact your commute, but you grab your umbrella on your way out the door just in case. This choice delivers a serotonin boost, because you now feel likely to be both on time and prepared.

However, this sequence can all too easily turn into a loop that, once it gets going, builds enough momentum to spiral out of control. A fearful thought triggers a fearful feeling, which then confirms the fearful thought, which deepens the feeling, and so on. You're chatting with someone at work and see them glance at their phone. That flicker of movement turns into the thought *Am I boring them?* This question triggers a pang of embarrassment, which prompts you to check your memory: *Am I a boring person?*

Your memory's negativity bias then kicks in (more on this in Chapter 8), disregarding the hundreds of times you've talked with people who were clearly engaged and enjoying your conversation, to remind you of a time in middle school, perhaps thirty-plus years ago, when someone made fun of you for something you said. Your cortisol levels rise. Your serotonin levels plummet. You feel like an unloved and incompetent social reject. You end the conversation quickly and rush back to your desk. The next time you see that person, you'll experience another negative dose.

CORTISOL AND THE FEAR RESPONSE

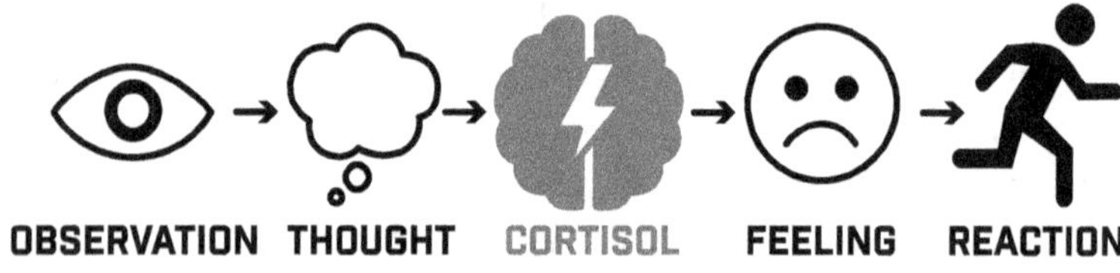

This is your brain trying to protect you. At the neurochemical level, there's no difference between a perceived (even if entirely imagined) threat to our social status and a panther attack. Because your brain is designed to keep you alive, not happy, it's not interested in your thriving—only in your survival. It remembers every detail of a negative encounter, and whenever you notice even one or two of those details again, it prepares you for a repeat of the encounter by releasing adrenaline and cortisol. Again, this response was helpful when it meant our ancestors remembered where the panthers lived. It's less useful in corporate hallways.

The crucial distinction here is it's not the coworker (or even the panther) who triggers a fear response. It's our *thoughts* about them. With the possible exception of loud noises and falling, we're not hardwired to be afraid of much.[11] If you want some difficult-to-watch but compelling proof, do an internet search for an episode of the Australian Broadcasting Corporation's episode of *Secret Science* called "Why Aren't Babies Scared of Snakes?"

There is nothing good or bad but thinking makes it so.
—**William Shakespeare**

Of course, there are plenty of things it's highly adaptive to be fearful of, or at least cautious of—hot stoves, highways, and heights spring to mind—but our overactive physiology gleefully adds things like public speaking, phone-checking colleagues, and financial ruin to the list. The irony here is that the more you fear, the less safe you become. Fear shuts down your prefrontal cortex, where reason and creativity live. It narrows your perspective and makes it harder to solve the very problem you're spiraling over. When you disrupt the thought-feeling-action loop, not only will you feel safer, you'll *be* safer—because you'll be more capable of finding an effective solution to your problems.

This is where intentional dosing meets mental agility. Dosing shifts your chemistry. Reframing shifts your narrative. Together, they create the space for something new to emerge.

---

11   Aditi Subramaniam, "The Neurobiology of Fear: How Much of Fear Is Inborn?," *Psychology Today,* Oct. 3, 2019, http://www.psychologytoday.com/us/blog/parenting-neuroscience-perspective/201910/the-neurobiology-fear.

TAKE A MOMENT
Recall the last time your thoughts spiraled into a stress loop. What was the initial trigger thought, and how could you reframe it?

THE TRIPLE R FRAMEWORK

The Triple R Framework is a powerful model I developed for navigating disruption, managing emotional states, and regaining agency in the face of uncertainty. It's a loop you can run again and again, especially when the hits keep coming. Unlike rigid prescriptions for productivity or positivity, this framework honors the emotional reality of disruption while creating a structure for recovery and forward movement. It's how you stabilize your chemistry so that your mind can accelerate again.

1. RECOGNIZE: NAME WHAT YOU FEEL

You've been disrupted—laid off, blindsided, derailed—and before you can move forward, you need to name what's happening inside you. That means not just acknowledging the external facts ("I lost my job") but identifying your internal reality ("I feel ashamed," "I'm afraid I'll never recover," "I'm grieving the loss of control").

By "recognizing," I mean stepping into the whole emotional truth of what you're experiencing. Emotions naturally peak and fade within about ninety seconds, unless we prolong them by adding stories, judgment, or resistance. If you can simply notice and name an emotion while staying present with it, you'll allow it to move through you like a wave. Of course, this isn't as easy as it may sound. Start by simply learning to name the basic "negative" emotions such as sad, angry, or scared. Often, that's enough. But you can use this "feelings wheel" to help you further refine your emotion-naming.

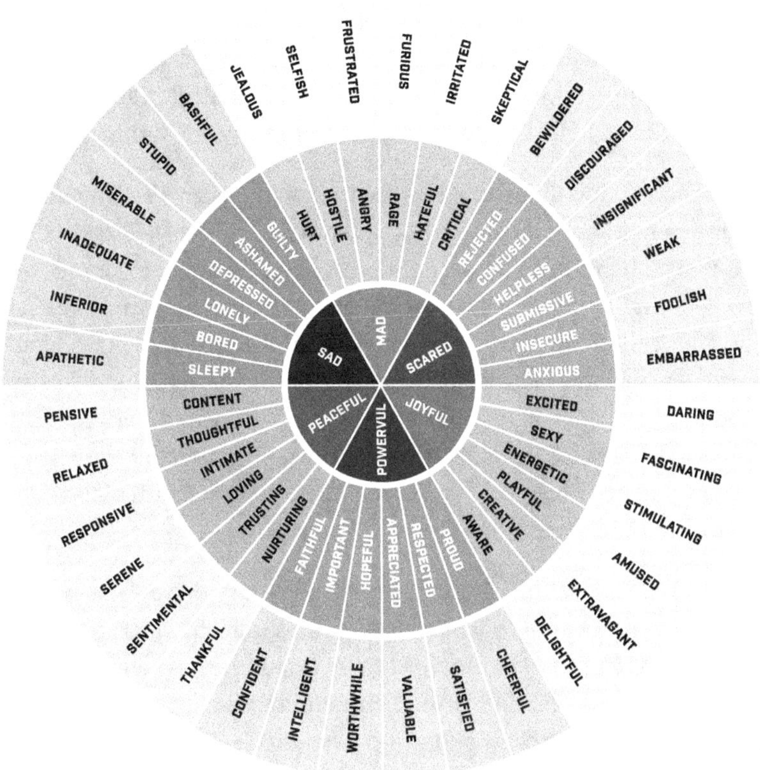

12

12   Gloria Willcox, "The Feeling Wheel: A Tool for Expanding Awareness of Emotions and Increasing Spontaneity and Intimacy," Dec. 28, 2017, https://doi.org/10.1177/036215378201200411, Creative Commons License (CC BY-SA 4.0) via Wikimedia Commons, https://commons.wikimedia.org/wiki/File:The_Feeling_Wheel.png.

2. RESET: SHIFT YOUR STATE

Once you've named what's going on, you'll reset your brain chemistry. Get yourself to neutral so that you can think clearly and act intentionally. DOSE yourself with small, thoughtful practices that release the right feel-good hormones in healthy, meaningful ways.

People occasionally worry that this kind of positive self-medication is inauthentic or unhealthy in some way. It isn't. First of all, you're probably already doing it with social media or ice cream, so you might as well be intentional about it. Second, sure, if you're dosing to bounce back from that phone-obsessed coworker, you may never reexperience the twinge of anxiety you felt. But if you're coping with a major disruption, have no fear: The negative emotions will come back, and that's okay. The goal here isn't permanent state change; it's just to give yourself enough positive mental room to make some material progress.

Think of it as shifting mental gears. You can't drive forward in reverse. Scrolling for dopamine hits or polishing off a quart of rocky road might feel good in the short term, but in the long term, you're likely to end up feeling worse. A more intentional neurochemical reset can give your body and mind what they actually need.

Most of the DOSEs below will work for any low mood, but if you want to get detail-oriented, you can zero in on which neurochemicals are bottoming out, as each leaves a kind of fingerprint on your feelings. When a particular neurochemical is running low, specific patterns tend to show up:

- **Low dopamine** levels can feel like apathy or aimlessness. You might struggle to get motivated, feel like nothing excites you, or bounce between distractions without finishing anything. It's the "blah" behind procrastination.

Want dopamine? Set micro-goals and chase them. Dopamine is about the pursuit, not the prize. Even folding laundry counts—if you track it and celebrate completion.

- **Low oxytocin** often manifests as feelings of loneliness or disconnection, even if you're not physically alone. You might feel isolated, emotionally numb, or suspicious of others' intentions. It's that "I'm on my own" feeling.

  Want oxytocin? Text a friend. Make eye contact. Hug your kid. Or get a dog—they're portable oxytocin machines.

- **Low serotonin** levels can manifest as irritability, low self-esteem, or feeling like you're stuck at the bottom of the social ladder. You might be unusually sensitive to rejection or feel like your efforts aren't being recognized.

  Want serotonin? Reflect on progress. Journal. Acknowledge your wins—even the tiny ones. Your brain doesn't know the difference between "I crushed a keynote" and "I finally organized my desktop." Anything that gives you a sense of accomplishment gives you serotonin. So do sunshine and green tea.

- **Low endorphins** show up as emotional heaviness or tension that doesn't release. You might feel physically depleted or emotionally fragile, as if everything is a little harder than it should be. Often, laughter or movement feels distant or unavailable.

  Want endorphins? Move your body. Laugh. Cry. Listening to music can release endorphins in your body, as can wine and spicy food.

If you're looking for a single source of most feel-good neurochemicals, dark chocolate is a good option.[13] Sex is better.[14]

3. REFRAME: CHOOSE THE THOUGHT THAT FUELS THE FEELING THAT FUELS THE ACTION

Only after you've reset can you choose meaningfully and consciously how to interpret the situation, thereby generating a more productive emotional state. In reframing, you change the thoughts that cause the feelings. In our phone-y coworker example, instead of assuming they're bored, you might reframe their glance at the screen by thinking, *They must have an upcoming meeting.* This reframe makes the event about something other than you, since, despite how it may feel, the vast majority of things are not. (We can blame the "spotlight effect," which makes people consistently believe they're being noticed more than they actually are, for this nifty mental trick.[15])

In a disrupted state, your brain will naturally jump to worst-case scenarios, assume negative intent, or catastrophize what's

---

13   Ji-Hee Shin et al., "Consumption of 85% Cocoa Dark Chocolate Improves Mood in Association with Gut Microbial Changes in Healthy Adults: A Randomized Controlled Trial," *The Journal of Nutritional Biochemistry* 99 (Jan. 2022): 108854, https://doi.org/10.1016/j.jnutbio.2021.108854.

14   Rocco S. Calabrò et al., "Neuroanatomy and Function of Human Sexual Behavior, A Neglected or Unknown Issue?," *Brain and Behavior* 9, no. 12 (Dec. 2019), https://doi.org/10.1002/brb3.1389.

15   Thomas Gilovich et al., "The Spotlight Effect in Social Judgment: An Egocentric Bias in Estimates of the Salience of One's Own Actions," *Journal of Personality and Social Psychology* 78, no. 2 (2000): 211–22, https://doi.org/10.1037/0022-3514.78.2.211.

happening. That's just evolution. However, you don't have to accept the thoughts you think.

Viktor Frankl, the Holocaust survivor and psychiatrist who wrote *Man's Search for Meaning*, famously said, "Everything can be taken from a man but one thing: the last of the human freedoms—to choose one's attitude in any given set of circumstances." That, with perhaps the substitution of the more inclusive "person" for "man," is the heart of reframing. You may not choose the disruption, but you can decide what it means to you. Remember, we're not afraid of snakes or failure; we're afraid because *of what we think about* a snake (*It will bite me*) or failure (*It will humiliate me*).

Reframing doesn't magically make things easy, but it does give you the emotional footing to move forward with strength, clarity, and purpose. Instead of *This reorganization is taking away a role I knew and was good at*, maybe the reframe is *I get to learn and grow through what's next, which will make me even more valuable in the future.* This new thought is a tiny nudge toward a better feeling, which enables better actions. If you think failure is proof that you're a loser, you're unlikely to try again. If you think it's a teacher or a forcing function, you're much more likely to put in the effort that leads to eventual success.

THE TRIPLE R FRAMEWORK

RECOGNIZE:
NAME WHAT YOU FEEL

You've been disrupted—laid off, blindsided, derailed—and before you can move forward, you need to name what's happening inside you.

RESET:
SHIFT YOUR STATE

Once you've named what's going on, you'll reset your brain chemistry. Get yourself to neutral so you can think clearly and act intentionally.

REFRAME:
CHOOSE THE THOUGHT THAT FUELS THE FEELING THAT FUELS THE ACTION

Only after you've reset can you choose meaningfully and consciously how to interpret the situation, thereby generating a more productive state.

TAKE A MOMENT

Identify one current disruption in your life. Write down answers to these questions: *What am I feeling?* (Recognize) *How can I adjust my neurochemistry?* (Reset) *What new story can I tell myself?* (Reframe)

MICRO AND MACRO

Research from Harvard Medical School shows that prolonged stress disrupts neural communication between the amygdala and prefrontal cortex, impairing the ability to regulate emotions and make thoughtful decisions.[16] Chronic stress also reduces cognitive flexibility and working memory, making it harder to switch perspectives or hold complex ideas in mind.

The Triple R Framework is a mental and emotional hygiene practice you can return to again and again to metabolize disruption and move forward. It's a micro-level habit with macro-level benefits. When practiced regularly, it raises your emotional baseline—your overall sense of well-being, resilience, and self-leadership that keeps you in a positive state even when life throws a curveball. You're less likely to crash when disruption hits if you've built up internal strength and perspective over time. You won't just feel better; you'll function better.

In the same way you wouldn't wait until you're dehydrated to start drinking water, don't wait until you're crashing to begin managing your neurochemistry. Start incorporating it into your day-to-day now, working on the micro to build the macro. In a world where chaos is constant, stability isn't something you stumble into; it's something you engineer, one DOSE at a time.

Disruption may hijack your brain, but you don't have to hand over the keys. You can upgrade your internal chemistry, interrupt the downward spiral, and steer yourself back toward clarity, creativity,

---

16   Amy F.T. Arnsten et al., "The Effects of Stress Exposure on Prefrontal Cortex: Translating Basic Research into Successful Treatments for Post-Traumatic Stress Disorder," *Neurobiology of Stress* 1 (2015): 89–99, https://doi.org/10.1016/j.ynstr.2014.10.002.

and control. Using DOSE and the Triple R Framework isn't self-indulgence; it's self-leadership. It's the difference between reacting impulsively and responding deliberately. In a world that won't slow down for your recovery, learning to regulate your internal state becomes not just helpful, but essential.

But knowing how to DOSE, recognize, reset, and reframe isn't the end of the story. It's the groundwork. Coupled with the 1440 Method, it's how you stabilize yourself enough to turn disruption into motion.

CHAPTER 5

THE STABILIZATION STACK

Nine months into what should have been the deal of a lifetime, I learned a valuable lesson about assumptions. I was part of a Lockheed Martin team sitting around a conference table in Georgia with representatives from the Canadian government. For nearly a year, my team had been developing a proposal to supply Canada with an aircraft training system and maintenance package valued at approximately $500 million. We'd built strong relationships with our Canadian counterparts, navigated multiple regulatory hurdles, and invested countless hours. We were finally sitting down to talk numbers.

Our presentation was flawless, but followed by a long, awkward pause. The Canadians looked surprised, almost shocked. "Um," their team lead said, "we don't have anywhere near $500 million. Not even half that."

I felt my stomach drop. How had we gotten nine months into this process and been so far off base?

Back at the hotel that evening, the finger-pointing began in earnest. My team was frustrated, stressed, and looking for someone to blame. We should have asked about budgets earlier. The Canadians *should* have been clearer about their constraints. There were plenty of reasons to be angry and plenty of blame to spread around. We "shouldn'd" all over ourselves.

When we reconvened the next day, it felt like walking into a blind date with an ex. The veneer of professionalism eroded quickly as people raised their voices and became increasingly frustrated. We were stuck in survival thinking, focusing on what had gone wrong, who was at fault, and why this was essentially an impossible situation.

The dynamic was starting to spiral into panic when something clicked. I realized I had a choice to make: I could join the rage and self-pity, or I could do something else. I stood up, looked around the room, and said, "Okay, everyone, let's get this figured out for our customer."

The room went quiet. You could practically hear the mental gears shifting. In that moment, something fundamental changed. Instead of dwelling on what had gone wrong and how much it had cost us, I refocused the team on what we were going to do about it and how we could still serve our customer. I wasn't dismissing the challenge—I was choosing to meet it head-on, in a spirit of faith and service.

Miraculously, it worked.

Over the next three months, we completely scrapped our original plan, got creative, found efficiencies, and ultimately figured out how to deliver a solution that met their needs for $193 million. That won us the contract.

Years later, my boss still brought up that moment and how the shift from blame to ownership transformed not just that meeting but the trajectory and outcome of the whole project.

THE FOUNDATION THAT MADE THE MOMENT

I was able to shift our collective gears only because I'd spent years building and stacking a set of tools I could call on in the moment.

The 1440 Method helped me get clear about my values, including my deep commitment to growth and helping others succeed. Even when everything felt chaotic, I knew what mattered most to me.

DOSE and the Triple R Framework enabled me to manage my mental state when the pressure was intense. When I felt that familiar cortisol spike of panic and frustration, I recognized it, reset my brain chemistry, and reframed the situation from "This is a complete disaster" to "This is an opportunity to lead."

The 1440 Method, DOSE, and the Triple R Framework aren't specialized tools but rather an integrated system for internal stability that allowed me to function at my best when external circumstances were at their worst.

When these practices work together, you don't just feel better; you function better.

In the moment, I was extremely stressed. And yes, my amygdala got thoroughly hijacked. But even with it halfway to Cuba, the foundational emotional stability I'd developed allowed me to settle my chemistry quickly and reclaim my prefrontal cortex, where my higher mind, broader perspectives, and leadership skills live.

Leaders can move from surviving disruption to leading through it by leveraging a values-focused, neuroscience-based stabilization stack.

HOW THE STACK WORKS

If leadership is a performance, stability is the stage. When things get disrupted, people may initially look up the org chart for direction, but if the nominal leader is spiraling, defensive, or emotionally depleted, whoever recovers their emotional equilibrium first becomes the de facto leader. Each of the stabilization stack's tools handles a different part of the system, but they work in concert to put you back in charge of yourself so that you're fit to lead others. Disruption stops being something you hope to survive and becomes a platform for you to play on.

THE STABILIZATION STACK'S THREE INTERLOCKING PIECES

The 1440 Method ensures your time reflects your values, not just your obligations. When you know what matters, you waste less energy on what doesn't and generate more serotonin, the neurochemical of stability and self-respect.

Intentional DOSE habits maintain a healthy level of access to these neurochemicals and reset your brain chemistry when stress spikes, helping shift your mental state from reactive to responsive, from adrenaline and cortisol to dopamine, oxytocin, serotonin, and endorphins.

The Triple R Framework (recognize, reset, reframe) helps you stay mentally agile when things go sideways. Before you spiral, you catch yourself and dial down the emotional intensity. Your rewired thought-feeling-action loop enables you to quickly enter a creative, problem-solving mindset, allowing you to think, feel, and act with less emotion and more wisdom.

WARNING SIGNS OF A SHAKY STACK

Keep an eye out for these signs that you need more stabilization:

- Time feels like it's managing you.
- Your calendar is packed, but you don't seem to be getting things done.

- You get things done, but they're the wrong things.
- Your time is spent in the "urgent, not important" quadrant of the Eisenhower matrix.[17]
- Minor disruptions feel major.
- You spend the night awake, thinking about what you wish you'd said yesterday.
- You're always exhausted.
- You find yourself snapping at people, making rushed decisions you later regret, or feeling like you can barely keep your head above water.
- You depend on fear to motivate you.
- Everything is someone else's fault.
- Everything is your fault.
- Everything feels like a crisis.
- You're self-medicating with food or Facebook, alcohol or Amazon, caffeine or credit cards, prescription meds or procrastination.

These behaviors aren't character defects; they're system failures—indications that your stabilization stack needs maintenance.

BEYOND STABILITY

Stability isn't the endgame. It's the foundation that makes everything else possible. After all, the world doesn't need more leaders who operate well when things are easy. We have plenty of those. The world needs leaders who can adapt by holding on (or quickly recovering) their highest human capabilities in the face of change and who will help others do the same.

---

17   This concept from a 1954 speech by President Dwight D. Eisenhower was popularized by Stephen Covey in *The 7 Habits of Highly Effective People* (Simon & Schuster, 1989).

The wise adapt themselves to circumstances,
as water molds itself to the pitcher.
—Chinese Proverb

To me, adaptability is an advanced form of resilience. Resilience allows you to go back to where you were, while adaptability helps you bounce forward to where you want to go. This definition owes a great deal to Stanford psychologist Carol Dweck's research on the growth mindset (a belief that your abilities and intelligence can evolve with effort and learning) and to Nassim Nicholas Taleb's concept of antifragility (systems and people grow stronger through stress, not despite it).[18,19]

Resilience is strong. Adaptability is flexible and, like physical flexibility, requires core strength. Adaptability isn't wishy-washy, unlike flexibility, which can be. Without a strong foundation, adaptability becomes just another kind of reactivity. You end up changing direction every time the wind shifts, not because you're being strategic but because every breeze is blowing you about.

The stabilization stack's 1440 Method provides clarity about your core values and priorities, those fundamentals that remain constant. DOSE and the Triple R Framework give you the tools to stay grounded when everything else is shifting. Together, they create the internal stability that makes external adaptability possible.

---

18   Carol Dweck, *Mindset: The New Psychology of Success* (Random House, 2006).

19   Nassim Nicholas Taleb, *Antifragile: Things That Gain from Disorder* (Random House, 2012).

Adaptability isn't the absence of chaos but rather the skill of staying centered in the middle of it. It's an ability that's built, not bestowed. When your minutes, your mindset, and your meaning are all aligned, you become the kind of leader people naturally want to follow—not because you're the loudest voice in the room but because you're the calmest presence in the eye of the storm.

CLARITY ⟶ CHEMISTRY ⟶ CONTROL

The 1440 Method gives you clarity. The ability to DOSE manages your chemistry. The three R's deliver control. When they work together, you're no longer trying to survive disruption; instead, you've created the stability that allows you to choose your responses to it.

PART 2

MOVE WITH PURPOSE

CHAPTER 6

EMBRACE UNCERTAINTY

In 1968, Spencer Silver, a scientist at 3M, set out to create a powerful new adhesive. He failed. His new formulation was a weak, pressure-sensitive glue that stuck lightly and released just as easily. For years, Silver tried to promote his invention inside the company but met with little success. There just wasn't much enthusiasm for an adhesive that didn't really adhere.

Then, in 1974, one of Silver's colleagues made a connection that changed everything. Art Fry had long been frustrated that his paper bookmarks kept slipping from the pages of his church hymnal and wondered if Silver's adhesive might solve the problem. Together, they refined the idea, producing small notes that would stick to paper without damaging it and could be repositioned easily and repeatedly.

The first market test in 1977, under the name "Press 'n Peel," was underwhelming. But 3M persisted. After an aggressive sampling campaign, Post-it Notes launched nationally in 1980 and became one of the company's most successful products.

When Silver's initial experiment failed to produce a new high-tack new glue, he didn't lose confidence in the utility of his new low-tack one. Why would anyone want such a thing? Who knew, but he talked about it to enough people that when Fry came across a use case for it, he knew who to call.

Of course, Silver didn't set out to fail. Not many healthy people do. Because we've been conditioned to believe failure reflects on our worth and competence, we chase certainty, seek control, and build elaborate plans to protect ourselves from things going wrong. But in a disrupted and disruptive world, that instinct can trap us in the very conditions we're trying to escape.

When circumstances change, clinging more tightly to your original plans won't restore your world to its original state. Resisting a setback keeps you from moving beyond it. Progress comes from accepting reality, stepping into uncertainty, letting go of the illusion of control, and being willing to learn as you go.

You can't harness the power of disruption by fighting it. The seven accelerators work by hoisting windmill blades into the storm. It may be frightening or even painful, but it's where the energy for growth lives.

It's our natural intuition to want to be certain and win all the time. The counterintuitive truth is that only when we embrace uncertainty can we navigate disruption and reach success.

FROM STABILIZATION TO GROWTH

In Part 1, we built your stabilization stack:

- **The 1440 Method** reminds you of what is changeless when everything else is shifting. Your clarity about values and priorities becomes your decision-making filter. It transforms uncertainty from "I don't know what to do" into "I don't know exactly how, but I know why."

- **DOSE practices** become your real-time regulation system when uncertainty triggers stress responses. Instead of letting fear hijack your prefrontal cortex, you have tools to quickly restore access to higher-order thinking.

- **The Triple R Framework** helps you interrupt the thought-feeling-action loop that turns uncertainty into paralysis.

Together, these tools create a useful, if paradoxical, stable uncertainty. Having the ability to remain grounded in your core while staying flexible in your responses is like being a tree with deep roots and branches that bend in the wind. It won't eliminate uncertainty, but it can give you the internal steadiness to navigate uncertainty skillfully.

Many leaders mistakenly think that once their stabilization stack is in place, the job is done. They retreat into what feels safe and familiar. They optimize existing systems, perfect current processes, and stay in their comfort zones.

But disruption doesn't care about your comfort zone. And growth doesn't happen there.

The transition from stabilization to growth requires a fundamental mindset shift: from seeking control to trusting your ability to adapt. It's the difference between trying to predict the rain and carrying an umbrella.

FROM REACTION TO ADAPTATION

When I work with leaders in the middle of disruption, I often hear some version of "I just want things to go back to normal." But disruption doesn't take you back. It invites you forward.

To move from disrupted to adaptable, you need two things:

1.   A mindset that accepts uncertainty as part of the process

2.   Micro-level control mechanisms that help you tolerate uncertainty and take the next step, even when the whole map isn't clear

Early in my leadership career, I made the mistake of treating every disruption like a fire drill: Move fast, fix the problem, and restore order. That worked well when the issue was small. However, as the changes got larger and more unpredictable—such as entire team restructures, client losses, and economic shifts—that strategy just caused leadership whiplash. The leaders who thrive in complexity aren't the ones who move fastest. They're the ones who *learn* fastest.[20]

THE LEARNING MINDSET VS. THE KNOWING MINDSET

Accepting uncertainty requires a fundamental shift from a knowing mindset to a learning mindset. The knowing mindset is a protection mechanism. We believe that knowing enough can save us from the risk of failure. But disruption breaks that contract. The path forward isn't knowable in advance, which means failure becomes inevitable—not as an end point, but as part of the navigation system.

The **knowing mindset** says, *I need to have the answer before I act. I should be able to predict outcomes. If I don't know what will happen, I shouldn't move forward.*

---

20   Northwestern University Society of Education and Social Policy, "Why Learning-Oriented Leaders Thrive," Aug. 25, 2025, https://sesp.northwestern.edu/graduate-professional/learning-and-organizational-change/knowledge-exchange/why-leaders-with-a-learning-orientation-thrive-in-complexity.html.

The **learning mindset** says, *I'll discover the answer through action. I'll gather information as I go. Forward movement generates the clarity I need.*

It's a language change that changes neurology. When you're in knowing mode, your brain focuses on pattern recognition and prediction. It works well in stable environments but becomes rigid when patterns break down. When you're in learning mode, your brain activates different neural networks associated with curiosity, experimentation, and adaptation.

I learned this distinction the hard way during my transition from Lockheed Martin to consulting. My engineering background had trained me to solve problems through analysis. I was comfortable gathering all available data, modeling potential outcomes, and then executing the optimal solution. But starting a business doesn't work like that. There's no complete dataset for "how to build a successful leadership development firm." I had to learn by doing, adjust based on feedback, and trust the process, even when I couldn't see the destination.

BUILDING UNCERTAINTY TOLERANCE

Like physical fitness, uncertainty tolerance is a muscle that strengthens with practice. You don't build it by jumping into chaos, but by exposing yourself to progressively more challenging situations.

Here's how to train this muscle systematically:

Start with micro-uncertainties. Look for small areas where you can practice acting without complete information. Try a new route to work, experiment with a different morning routine, or test a new approach in a low-stakes meeting. The goal isn't dramatic change—it's building comfort with the unknown.

Design learning experiments. Instead of committing to massive change, design small tests. If you're considering a career shift, informational interviews are learning experiments. If you're considering a new business strategy, a small pilot is a valuable learning experiment. Frame these as research, not permanent decisions.

Separate action from outcome. Rather than engineering perfect results, focus on taking the next right step. The 1440 Method helps here—when you're clear on your values and direction, you can move forward even when the path is unclear.

Practice rapid iteration. Set shorter feedback loops. Instead of six-month plans, try six-week (or even six-day) experiments. Instead of annual reviews, do weekly check-ins. The faster you can collect information and adjust, the more comfortable you'll become with uncertainty.

Celebrate discovery, not just success. Track what you learn, not just what you achieve. Did the experiment fail but teach you something valuable? That's a win. Did you take action despite fear? That's a win. Celebrating these wins reinforces the learning mindset.

WHY UNCERTAINTY FEELS LIKE DANGER

It's not the unknown that scares us about uncertainty but rather the fear of what might happen. If you knew every uncertain situation would turn out well, just not exactly how, life would be one big happy surprise. The unknown would be an adventure, not a threat. It's the possibility that the unknown will include pain and failure that makes mere uncertainty enough to trigger our entire threat-response system.

Our brains are remarkably efficient at this equation:

Unknown Outcome = Potential Failure = Danger

It's why you can intellectually know that a new opportunity is good for your career but still feel that knot in your stomach. Your nervous system isn't evaluating the opportunity; it's scanning for failure risk.

Here's the problem with that lens: We try to engineer certainty to avoid failure, but the very act of seeking certainty keeps us in spaces where the stakes are low and growth is limited.

The leaders who thrive in disruption aren't the ones who've eliminated failure risk. They're the ones who've accepted that uncertainty and failure are a package deal—and decided the potential upside is worth proceeding anyway. Their organizations thrive accordingly.

I'm sure you've heard this famous question: What would you do if you could not fail? It's meant to be freeing, and it is, but it's also a fantasy. Failure is always possible. So maybe the better question is this: What matters enough that you'd be willing to fail? That shift—from seeking guaranteed success to choosing worthy uncertainty—is what makes self-disruption possible.

Does that sound like a bad thing? Let me explain.

MAKING YOUR OWN HEAVY WEATHER

Until now, we've been talking about how to respond when disruption finds you. But what about the times when you decide to create a little disruption yourself? It may sound like inviting a hurricane into your living room, but deliberately shaking up your own habits and structures can be one of the fastest ways to grow.

There are two levels where this matters: personal and organizational.

PERSONAL SELF-DISRUPTION

One of the earliest times I disrupted myself on purpose was while working at Lockheed Martin. We were about to build the first aircraft in a new production lot. Buried in the data, I noticed something alarming: Close to two hundred design changes were scheduled for that single plane. Each change was being managed separately, with its own engineer and its own deadlines—yet the expectation was that we'd build this aircraft faster and cheaper than the one before it. To me, it looked like a train wreck in slow motion.

I had two options: stay in my lane and hope someone else sorted it out, or raise my hand. I'd been starting to feel a little bored with my job, so I chose the latter. I went to my boss and asked if I could put together a project team to coordinate all the changes. He agreed, I pulled in people from across the organization, and we started meeting weekly to collect all the relevant data in one place and track progress as a team.

A few months later, when the program's vice president raised the same concern, my boss was able to say, "Andre's already working on it." That work was elevated, my boss made me his deputy, and eventually, our team won a Lockheed Martin Aerostar Award for keeping the whole effort on track.

I didn't have to take that assignment. Nobody asked me to. But stepping into it stretched my skills, expanded my network, and showed me that sometimes the surest way to grow is to volunteer for the mess everyone else is avoiding. That's the essence of personal self-disruption. It might look like taking on a project outside your expertise, trying a lateral move, or putting yourself in a room where you're not the most knowledgeable person. The pattern is the same: Step into discomfort, get rattled, and discover something new.

CORPORATE INTRAPRENEURSHIP

Organizations can practice the same thing at scale. I've seen companies launch internal innovation labs that exist for one reason: to test wild ideas quickly. The goal isn't polished success. It's structured experimentation.

This is where "intelligent failures" come in. Instead of punishing teams when a new idea doesn't work, the best leaders design systems to capture the learning and redeploy it. "Fail fast" stops being a slogan and becomes a laboratory principle.

Corporate self-disruption can also look like encouraging cross-functional rotations, funding small side projects, or running "innovation sprints" where the only target outcome is team learning, not building a blockbuster. These efforts send a clear signal that says, "We don't just tolerate uncertainty; we cultivate it."

When leaders foster self-disruption inside their companies, they create a culture that not only survives disruption from outside but also productively generates it from within.

WHY FAILURE FEELS SO PERSONAL—AND WHY IT'S LYING

We tend to treat setbacks and failures as a referendum on our identity. If something we lead fails, we believe it says something about who we are, not just what we did.

But that belief is more cultural than factual. In many environments, particularly in traditional corporate settings, failure gets framed as incompetence rather than experimentation or a setback along the path to success. That conditioning trains us to avoid risks and penalizes the very thing innovation depends on: learning.

You don't have to carry that cultural baggage. One way to shake it loose is to consciously separate the story you're telling from the facts on the ground. For example:

Old Belief	New Reframe
I need to be certain before I act.	I act to discover what works.
Failure is a threat to my reputation.	Setbacks are a part of the growth cycle.
Being wrong means I'm not good enough.	Being wrong means I'm progressing and learning.
If I fail, people won't trust me.	If I'm honest about failure, people will trust me more.

Changing your internal narrative doesn't make disruption easy, but it does make it survivable. And it keeps you from compounding the pain by turning every failure into a character flaw.

MEET YOUR INNER SABOTEURS

One reason it's so hard to accept setbacks is that we're battling not just external pressures but also our own internal voices. I borrow the names of three of Shirzad Chamine's ten saboteurs for this kind of self-talk:[21]

---

21   Shirzad Chamine, *Positive Intelligence: Why Only 20% of Teams and Individuals Achieve Their True Potential AND HOW YOU CAN ACHIEVE YOURS* (Greenleaf Book Group Press, 2012), 17.

- **The Hyper-Achiever** makes your value conditional on your success.

- **The Avoider** convinces you it's better to delay action than risk imperfection.

- **The Judge** criticizes you no matter what you do.

These saboteurs thrive in uncertainty. The more disrupted life feels, the louder they get. They are fear-based and cause doubt, comparison, and perfectionism. They're not evil, and they don't wish you harm—they just want you to be safe. And they define "safe" as whatever is familiar. Our brains aren't that interested in joy or growth. They just want not-dead. The trick is finding a way to make the bold, exciting, and unfamiliar feel *safe enough* to sneak in under the radar. We can't eliminate fear, but we can act while afraid if we manage the fear.

One executive I worked with had a Judge saboteur who was so loud that the poor woman couldn't get through a single day without second-guessing every choice she made. When we gave it a name and a persona (she called it "The Critic in the Corner"), she was able to put some distance between herself and that frightened voice. She didn't have to make it go away—she just had to stop letting it drive the bus.

I often tell clients: Notice the voice; then choose the action. You don't have to silence the saboteur to move forward. You just have to stop taking its advice. (If you're interested in learning more about these three saboteurs or their seven compatriots, I highly recommend Chamine's *Positive Intelligence*.)

Sometimes, leaders I work with mistake these toxic voices for internalized coaching, but there's a fundamental difference between criticizing yourself and holding yourself accountable.

Self-criticism sounds like this:

- *I'm stupid and a waste, and I never do anything right.*
- *Everything is all my fault.*
- *I "fell off" with my routine/discipline.*
- *Everyone is doing better than I am and has it all together.*

Self-accountability sounds like this:

- *What can I learn about myself from what happened?*
- *What pattern brought me here?*
- *I was human, and routine is always available to me.*
- *Humans are messy, and I work to consistently forgive myself.*

You are allowed to be both a masterpiece and a work in progress.
—Sophia Bush

By taking a compassionate and forgiving approach to yourself, you can cultivate a learning mindset and increase your resilience in the face of disruption.

FAILURE IS THE ONLY WAY FORWARD

In the leadership development world, there's a saying: Growth requires action, action invites failure, and failure provides feedback. Put another way: You can't think your way into transformation.

I used to want the complete blueprint before I made a move. I'd tell myself I was being strategic, but really, I was avoiding risk. It took me a while to realize that trying to outthink failure is itself a means of failing. You have to act your way into clarity.

We see this truth clearly in entrepreneurship. The startups that iterate quickly, test early, and treat failure as just a setback are the ones that evolve. Those that wait until everything is perfect usually miss the window. It's the same in leadership: You build momentum not by having the answer but by being willing to find it through action.

That doesn't mean throwing spaghetti at the wall. It means moving forward with purpose, knowing that failure isn't a detour—it's part of the path.

READING + REPS

Small practices to build your tolerance for uncertainty

You don't need to upend your life to build resilience. Big shifts are built on small experiments. Below are nine practical ways to apply this chapter's insights today.

1. RUN A MICRO-TEST

Pick one decision you've been overthinking. Instead of searching for the "right" answer, define a micro-experiment you can run this week. What's one small action that could give you more information? Set a date, take the step, and log what you learn.

2. USE THE LANGUAGE OF LEARNING

When you catch yourself thinking, *I should already know this*, reframe it to *I'm learning how to do this*. Shift *I need to get this right* to *I'm running an experiment*. Language rewires mindset—and mindset shapes outcomes.

3. TALK BACK TO A SABOTEUR

Identify the internal saboteur voice that's loudest right now. Is it your Hyper-Achiever, Avoider, or Judge? Write down what it's saying. Then, write a response from your grounded self. Practice choosing enlightened action over obedience to that voice.

4. SHARE A FAILURE—AND THE LESSON

Normalize failure on your team or in your peer circle by going first. Share a recent misstep and what it taught you. Ask others what they've learned from their own setbacks. Vulnerability lowers fear and builds trust.

5. ROTATE YOUR ROUTINE

Choose one daily or weekly habit you've been running on auto-pilot—your meeting format, your workout, even your commute. Change it deliberately. Pay attention to what you notice about yourself and others when you break your own pattern.

6. VOLUNTEER FOR A STRETCH PROJECT

Look for an assignment or opportunity that feels just outside your comfort zone. Raise your hand. Don't wait until you feel "ready." Growth rarely sends a calendar invite.

7. SHADOW OUTSIDE YOUR LANE

Ask to sit in on a different department's meeting or spend an afternoon with a colleague who has a role you know little about. Treat it like a field trip. New contexts spark new ideas.

8. PITCH A MINI-EXPERIMENT AT WORK

Propose a small test to your team: a new way of running a meeting, piloting a product idea, or experimenting with customer feedback loops. Frame it as a learning sprint, not a permanent change.

9. HOST A "FAILURE PARTY"

Schedule fifteen minutes with your team (or even just a colleague) to share one experiment that didn't work out—and what you learned from it. Bonus points if you make it lighthearted. Nothing disarms fear of failure faster than laughter.

EMBRACING UNCERTAINTY

If you're navigating disruption right now, good. That means you're no longer stuck in the illusion of certainty. You're in the real world, where growth lives. You don't need to have all the answers. You don't need to be fearless. You just need to keep going.

The practices we've discussed (accepting uncertainty, reframing failure, noticing your saboteurs, and running micro-experiments) are how you start to build your "keep going" muscle. They teach you to act while afraid, learn while stumbling, and separate your identity from the outcome.

Once you've built that foundation, you can go further: You can disrupt yourself. Volunteering for a stretch assignment, piloting an experiment, or deliberately shaking up your habits is like lifting heavier weights once you've mastered the form. It's risky, but it's also an exponential growth accelerant. The same principle applies at the organizational level. Cultures that practice self-disruption from within generate change, rather than being surprised by it.

It may be your natural intuition, even your biology, to want to be right and do things well. But when you accept failure as feedback, embrace uncertainty as fuel, and even create your own storms when the skies look too calm, you don't just adapt—you grow.

CHAPTER 7

PUT "WHY" OVER "WHAT"

Several years ago, I went on a mission trip to Niger, Africa. I didn't know it at the time, but I was about to be disrupted in the best possible way.

Far from home, away from titles and to-do lists and everyone who knew me as "the executive" or "the engineer," I started to hear my thoughts a little more clearly. As a Christian, for me, this was a very powerful "God moment."

What I heard—what kept echoing in the stillness—wasn't a grand vision or a five-point plan. It was a simple, pressing question: *Why am I here?* Not in Niger, but on the earth. It was also a deeply disruptive question.

At that point in my life, I had accumulated a list of achievements, degrees, promotions, and deliverables that I was proud of. But that trip made me realize those were answers to a different kind of question. They were all "whats," not "whys." I could discuss what I had done, what I was currently working on, and what I wanted to achieve next. I couldn't say why.

In a single moment of clarity, I came to understand that my real purpose was to develop people. I felt called to invest in others and help them grow. That newfound understanding led me to start a mentoring program when I got back to the States. At the time, my job as an engineering director included leading a team of more than two thousand people, so I focused on their development as my primary role. Later, the experience gave me the courage to shift from engineering to leadership development as my career. Eventually, it became the foundation of my consulting business.

Disruption doesn't just shake things up out there; it creates space *in here*. It frees you to reflect on whether the life you're living matches what you believe matters most. Purpose, I've found, isn't something you discover once and check off a list. It's something you return to. It's something you refine and reconnect with, especially in times of change—because when the world shifts, the question isn't just "What do I do now?" but "Why does it matter?"

It's our natural intuition to set goals and focus on what we want, but the counterintuitive truth is that understanding why we want it is the only source of fortitude to push through both current and future disruptions.

WHY "WHY" MATTERS

Early in my career, I focused on "whats"—what role I wanted next, what promotion I was working toward, what project I needed to deliver. It was the way I had excelled in school and sports, and for the first several years of my professional life, that focus served me well. My success came from setting goals and hitting them. I defined my objectives, broke them down into tasks, and executed them. That's what high performers do, right? They "plan the work and work the plan."

But disruption doesn't care about your plans. It shows up uninvited in the form of reorganizations, layoffs, pandemics, and personal loss, rendering all your tidy goal-setting frameworks useless. So *what's* left?

Exactly.

Why is different from *what*. It doesn't get shaken by circumstance. It's not tied to a job description or an org chart. Your "why" is the deeper reason that gives you direction and your work meaning, even when the map changes.

He who has a why to live for can bear almost any how.
—Friedrich Nietzsche

Despite being an engineer by training and profession, my "why" has always been about people. When I left Lockheed Martin after nearly two decades climbing the ladder, I understood that what fulfilled and energized me most wasn't the technical work. It was mentoring, coaching, and developing others. Not only did that insight help me figure out what to do next, it deepened my understanding of the situation and gave me the confidence and courage to build something new.

This deeper "why" is what I mean when I talk about purpose. It's the throughline that gives your life and leadership coherence, no matter what else changes.

THE PROBLEMS OF PURPOSE

When people start thinking about purpose, they often look for it in the wrong places or get stuck in what I call "purpose traps"—patterns that appear to be progress but quietly disconnect them from what truly matters. Let's take a quick tour of the traps and then dive into better ways to identify your purpose.

THE ROLE TRAP

"What do you do?" is often code for "Who are you?" It's easy to equate your job with your identity, particularly if you have a prestigious or high-paying job. But roles are temporary. They can be changed, restructured, outsourced, or retired. A sense of purpose needs to come from more than a job title.

If you overly identify with what you do, it becomes hard to know who you are when your work changes or disappears. Instead of asking, "What do I do?" try asking, "What do I bring?" Skills and titles may evolve. Your unique contribution is much more likely to remain constant.

YOUR PURPOSE IS YOUR REASON, NOT YOUR ROLE.

THE OUTCOME TRAP

This is the trap most likely to catch high achievers who define themselves by the results they deliver. When the outcomes are strong, you feel good. When they aren't, you feel lost. But if your sense of purpose depends on external success metrics, it's vulnerable to every disruption.

The outcome trap is one manifestation of what psychologist Carol Dweck, whom I mentioned briefly in the discussion of adaptability, refers to as having a fixed mindset. A fixed mindset associates identity with performance rather than effort, growth, and learning. (*I'm a winner*, or *I'm a loser.*) A growth mindset, on the other hand, focuses on effort, privileging process over outcome. (*I worked hard and won, and I'll keep working hard*, or *I worked hard but lost, and I'll keep working hard.*) A growth mindset fosters psychological safety, enabling individuals to explore, fail, and improve, even when the scoreboard isn't cooperating.[22]

YOUR PURPOSE IS A PROCESS, NOT AN OUTCOME.

THE REACTION TRAP

The last trap is less obvious but just as dangerous. It's the habit of making quick decisions without taking time to reflect. Sometimes, the pain of uncertainty is so great that we'll accept an inferior option just to settle the doubt. You get laid off, so you take the first job that shows up. A project ends, so you start something new out of urgency rather than clarity.

This kind of reaction might create activity, but it rarely leads to alignment. Without space to pause and reassess, you end up drifting further from your values. The to-do list stays full, but the meaning starts to leak out.

You can test whether this trap has you in its teeth by asking yourself whether the action you're taking is something you would have preferred to do had the disruption not happened. Would you have taken that first job if you were still fully employed? Is this project something you feel pulled by purpose to do, or do you feel more pushed by pressure?

YOUR PURPOSE IS ON PURPOSE, NOT ON IMPULSE.

---

22   Dweck, *Mindset*.

PURPOSE, PROFESSION, AND THE POWER TO CHOOSE

When I was considering leaving corporate life to start my own business, I shared the idea of following my purpose with a senior executive I deeply respected. His response caught me off guard. "Your purpose is to take care of your family," he told me in a tone that made it clear anything I desired beyond that responsibility was irrelevant.

At first, it made sense. Of course, providing for my family is part of my purpose. But something about that statement didn't sit right with me. Did it not matter whether I felt fulfilled by my work? Could there not be more?

His comment sent me into a period of deep reflection about work, family, and identity. I wrestled with the idea of purpose. Was it singular? Should it align with my profession? If we spend over a third of our waking lives working, shouldn't that time reflect what matters most to us?

My father didn't have the luxury of asking these questions. He worked the same job for thirty-three years, out of not passion but necessity. He showed up, provided, and disappeared inside a role he never wanted. His sacrifice allowed me a different path and the opportunity to pursue both responsibility and fulfillment.

Through that journey, I ask myself a modified version of the questions that make up the Japanese *ikigai* framework to clarify my purpose:

- *What am I good at?*

- *What do I care about?*

- *What does the world need?*

Answering these questions revealed clues that led to a purpose statement: My purpose is to change lives by helping people reach their full potential through purpose-driven leadership.

But it didn't solve the dilemma created by my mentor's assertion that my purpose was strictly to take care of my family. Purpose is about the contribution we want to make as well as the burden we naturally feel an obligation to carry. I realized purpose isn't singular—it's situational. I choose how to express it based on context. With my family, for example, I might express my purpose by waking up before I want to, in order to work out with my daughter and help her reach her full potential. This shift in thinking cost nothing but changed everything. It unleashed my purpose and was profoundly empowering.

THE CEO OF ME, INC.

Most people don't stumble onto purpose fully formed. They assemble it from patterns. What problems have always interested you? What kinds of people do you feel called to serve? What gives you energy, even when it's hard?

Psychologist Dan McAdams, who studies narrative identity, has shown that reflecting on personal stories helps us make sense of who we are and why we're here. The stories you tell about your most meaningful moments aren't just memories. They're signals pointing toward the kind of impact you want to have.[23]

You don't have to overhaul your entire life to live with purpose. Instead, start noticing the themes that already exist, and bring

---

23   Dan P. McAdams, "The Psychology of Life Stories," *Review of General Psychology* 5, no. 2 (2001): 100–22.

them into sharper focus. The job you're in might not be your dream role, but can you incorporate more of your values into how you show up? Look for small ways to serve your "why" right where you are. Part of what makes purpose powerful is that it doesn't rely on perfect conditions. It simply requires your attention and a willingness to act.

You are the CEO of Me, Inc. You have the power to choose which organizations, jobs, and projects align with your purpose—not the other way around. When your "why" is clear, your "what" becomes more impactful. That's when performance deepens. That's when resilience rises.

At the end of our careers, what matters most won't be metrics or milestones. It will be the people we impacted. Purpose isn't found in helping businesses—it's found in helping people.

So get clear. Choose courage. And build a life where purpose and profession walk side by side.

PURPOSE IS A DIRECTION, NOT A DESTINATION.

STAYING ROOTED WHEN ROLES SHIFT

Disruption often changes our roles or duties, but it doesn't have to change our purpose. In fact, some of the most purpose-driven seasons of life occur when old structures fall away, forcing us to ask, *Who am I without this title or those responsibilities I no longer have?*

If your purpose is tied to something fragile—like position, prestige, or performance—it will always feel at risk. But if it's tied to contribution, growth, and service, it becomes something you can carry with you no matter where you go.

Your job may change. Your team may change. The industry may change. But the essence of what you bring—the way you empower others, solve problems, spark ideas, or hold space—can remain a steady throughline.

That's what it means to lead with purpose—not just when things are going well, but especially when they aren't.

TAKE A MOMENT

Ask yourself: *What's the impact I want to make, regardless of job description? What values do I want to embody, even in transition?* **When you get clear on those answers, you stop waiting for the next opportunity to define you and instead bring your own definition into every room.**

READING + REPS

A daily purpose alignment ritual that helps you keep putting "why" over "what"

One of the best ways to stay connected to purpose is through small, consistent check-ins. All you need are a few quiet minutes and a willingness to be honest.

In the morning, ask yourself: *What would it look like to live my purpose today? What impact do I want to make and on whom? What problem do I want to solve?* It could be mentoring someone, showing up with integrity in a tough meeting, or staying present with your family after work. Write it down. Purpose doesn't have to be dramatic, just deliberate.

Midday, take a short break to peek at your list and ask yourself if you're still on track. If not, it's not too late to adjust.

In the evening, reflect on whether you lived in alignment with what matters most to you. If you did, acknowledge it. If not, don't be too hard on yourself. Get curious about what might have gotten in the way and how you might do things differently tomorrow. Document this self-reflection in a journal.

Don't allow any of these actions to take more than five minutes. As behavioral scientist BJ Fogg points out in *Tiny Habits*, it's often the smallest changes that make the biggest impact.[24] When these check-ins become part of your rhythm, they start to reshape how you move through the day. They reconnect your actions to your values and, over time, create confidence, clarity, and resilience.

PUTTING "WHY" OVER "WHAT"

It's our natural intuition to set goals and focus on what we want. Many of us have been taught to do so since grade school. The counterintuitive truth is that only knowing why we want it will give us the fortitude to persevere and the internal fulfillment we seek on the journey.

Disruption has a way of stripping things down to their essence. Titles, timelines, and tactics may fall away. But purpose can stay.

When you know your "why," you gain something rare in a changing world: direction without rigidity. You're able to respond instead of reacting and pivot without losing your footing. You can move through (and even dance with) chaos with intention, because you've already chosen the kind of person you want to be in its midst.

____

24   BJ Fogg, *Tiny Habits: The Small Changes That Change Everything* (Houghton Mifflin Harcourt, 2019).

That's the purpose advantage. It's not about having all the answers. It's about having something solid to return to when the answers change.

And in leadership—especially now—that clarity offers a competitive edge. People follow grounded leaders who live their values and consistently show up when everything else feels unstable.

So, if you're in a moment of disruption, don't just ask, "What's next?" Start by asking, "What still matters to me?" That's where the rebuilding begins.

CHAPTER 8

ENGINEER YOUR STRENGTHS

When I first started working with John, he was a senior technologist focused on engineering at a major tech company. On paper, he was exactly where he was supposed to be. He had a great title, in a cutting-edge field, with plenty of runway. But our conversations kept circling back to a deeper issue: He wanted to align what he did with who he was.

Early on, it was clear to me that John's real strength wasn't his unique skill set or technical expertise. It was the way he approached learning. John could pick up a new concept, turn it around in his mind, and find unexpected ways to apply it. That's who he was. The value of that skill became even more obvious halfway through our work together, when he applied to a graduate program at Harvard focused on business innovation—and got in, of course.

Just a few months later, though, his company shifted strategy, and John got swept up in the layoffs. Instead of fixating on what he had lost, he looked ahead.

Foreseeing that the next wave of transformation would happen in artificial intelligence, he dove in. He read, experimented, built side projects, and treated what could have been a fallow year like an immersive field study. He reinvented himself not by fixing weaknesses but by doubling down on his greatest strength: being a strategic learner. By the time the dust settled, he wasn't just employable again; he'd made himself essential. The company that had let him go came calling, this time with a more senior title and a broader mandate: AI architect.

John's story elegantly flips the usual script. Rather than going straight into diagnosis mode, scanning for what went wrong, looking for where he fell short, and figuring out what he needed to fix to get things back on track, he leveraged what he was best at and figured out how his strengths might matter even more in a disrupted work world.

In other words, John didn't become a different person; he became more of who he already was. And that's what positioned him to lead in the future rather than chase the past. Growth doesn't come from closing gaps. It comes from widening strengths.

That might sound counterintuitive, especially if you've sat through performance reviews focused on your "areas for improvement." It's easy to get so focused on leveling up weaknesses that you never stop to think about where you're already naturally strong. In times of uncertainty, your edge lies not in your patched weaknesses but in knowing what your unique strengths are and how to deploy them in different contexts. When you operate from your strengths, you're more effective, energized, and engaged—and more likely to create opportunities to do more of what you do best.

It's our natural intuition to focus on correcting our deficiencies. The counterintuitive truth is that the only way to bring out our best is to give most of our focus to honing and applying our natural strengths.

STRENGTH VS. WEAKNESS

Gallup's research across more than forty-five countries shows that strengths-based leadership improves morale, profits, sales, and customer satisfaction.[25] People whose work calls on their strengths daily are six times more likely to be engaged at work and three times more likely to report an excellent overall quality of life.[26] Yet only 20 percent of employees in large organizations say they have the opportunity to use their strengths every day.[27] That means four out of five people are showing up, putting in the hours, and never getting to operate from the part of themselves that's most powerful, effective, and fulfilling.

Perhaps this situation is a legacy of the Industrial Revolution, when the first managerial jobs developed to solve problems on the assembly line. In that context, it made sense to focus on the places where things broke down. Today, it often no longer makes sense, but especially in traditional corporate settings, feedback still tends to focus on what is suboptimal.

Don't get me wrong: I'm all about improvement, but when we over-rotate on what needs improvement, we start to believe that growth is purely about fixing weaknesses instead of amplifying

---

25   James K. Harter et al., "The Relationship Between Engagement at Work and Organizational Outcomes: 2020 Q12® Meta-Analysis," Gallup, Oct. 2020, https://media-01.imu.nl/storage/happyholics.com/6345/gallup-2020-q12-me-ta-analysis.pdf.

26   Peter Flade et al., "Employees Who Use Their Strengths Outperform Those Who Don't," Gallup, Oct. 8, 2015, https://www.gallup.com/workplace/236561/employees-strengths-outperform-don.aspx.

27   Laura Morgan Roberts et al., "How to Play to Your Strengths," *Harvard Business Review*, January 2005, https://hbr.org/2005/01/how-to-play-to-your-strengths.

strengths. Too often, we treat our highest contributions as baseline expectations and our flaws as the main event.

Psychologists call this tendency to pay more attention to what's wrong than what's right "negativity bias." It's an instinct that served humans well when we needed to scan the savanna and pay more attention to predators than pretty trees. In today's world, it delivers a triple whammy, because it means that management is more likely to see and pay attention to our weaknesses than our strengths, that we remember criticism more than praise, and that we internalize negative feedback more deeply. In fact, one researcher found that people tend to remember four negative memories for every one positive one.[28] It's no wonder people can rattle off a list of what they're not good at in an instant but struggle to name their top strengths.

WHAT STRENGTHS ARE

We tend to think of strengths as obvious skills like public speaking, strategic thinking, or technical expertise. Those are certainly valuable abilities, but often, your most intrinsic strengths aren't so apparent. They're the abilities you reach for without thinking, the knowledge you've internalized, and the traits most closely aligned with your values. They're how you move through the world when you're at your best.

In fact, strengths often appear so naturally that they go unrecognized as such. You may mistake them for your personality or disregard them because they feel effortless. However, the things that

---

28   Roy F. Baumeister et al., "Bad Is Stronger Than Good," *Review of General Psychology* 5, no. 4 (2001): 323–70, https://doi.org/10.1037/1089-2680.5.4.323.

                                    DISRUPTED

come most easily to you are often the things that others find difficult and make you valuable to your team.

Even when we are aware of something we do well, we tend to dismiss it—not because everyone is equally skilled but because the more skilled someone is, the more likely they are to underestimate their ability. Psychologists call this cognitive bias the Dunning-Kruger effect. People often misjudge their areas of excellence because their extraordinary ability feels ordinary to them. The more naturally you do something, the less likely you are to recognize it as a strength.[29]

But when we tap into those strengths regularly, our brains expand. Psychologist Barbara Fredrickson has shown that positive emotions we experience when using our strengths, such as joy, curiosity, and pride, broaden our awareness and build long-term psychological resources.[30] They expand our creativity, increase our resilience, and improve our ability to connect with others.

STRENGTHS AREN'T JUST ABILITIES; THEY'RE CATALYSTS.

That positive growth is especially important during disruption. When everything around you feels shaky, you need something

---

29   Justin Kruger and David Dunning, "Unskilled and Unaware of It," *Journal of Personality and Social Psychology* 77, no. 6 (1999): 1121–34, https://doi.org/10.1037//0022-3514.77.6.1121.

30   Barbara L. Fredrickson, "The Role of Positive Emotions in Positive Psychology: The Broaden-and-Build Theory of Positive Emotions," *American Psychologist* 56, no. 3 (2001): 218–26, https://doi.org/10.1037/0003-066X.56.3.218.

solid to stand on. Your strengths give you that foundation. They help you move from survival mode into contribution mode, from "What do I need to fix?" to "How can I serve?" And the moment you start operating from that place of clarity, confidence, and contribution, you're no longer just weathering disruption. You're capitalizing on it.

SEE YOUR STRENGTHS

To make the most of your strengths—and thus of whatever disruption you're experiencing—you first need to identify them. That sounds obvious, but most of us struggle to name our gifts. Four excellent tools can help you determine your strengths: testing the intersection of ability and energy, noticing what you do spontaneously, hearing what others say about you, and discovering what you can't not do.

ABILITY + ENERGY = STRENGTH

Perhaps the simplest indicator of a strength is the combination of energy and ability. Anything you're good at that gives you energy is a strength. We can think about the intersection of ability and energy in a four-quadrant Strengths Grid.

	Energy Drain	**Energy Source**
High Ability	Duty	Strength
Low Ability	Chore	Hobby

Duties are those things that we're good at but don't enjoy. They're the tasks people count on you to do that are boring, tedious, or mildly irritating.

Strengths are activities that aren't necessarily easy but provide you with a sense of satisfaction, even with that "This is what I was made for" feeling.

Chores are duties that wear you out. They may not be technically difficult, but they play to a weakness or require more intense external motivation.

Hobbies are those activities you enjoy in which your skill level isn't crucial to your enjoyment. You may be working toward mastery or simply engaging in it with no goal beyond that engagement.

TAKE A MOMENT

Consider the times when you feel most energized and vital. Try to remember times in the past when you felt most alive. Over the next week, check in with yourself two or three times a day and record anything that gives you a sense of competence or a boost of energy.

SPONTANEITY

Another powerful clue to your strengths is spontaneity, not in the sense of being impulsive but rather noticing those things you do naturally, without needing direction, prompting, or permission.

What do you find yourself doing before anyone asks? What kinds of problems do you instinctively lean toward solving? When the group is stuck, what role do you quietly slide into? These are signals.

Are you the one who steps in to mediate when tension rises, who frames the big picture when everyone's stuck in the weeds, or who notices what's not being said and asks the question that shifts the whole conversation? Are you the parent other people's kids talk to, or the one who always has the Band-Aids or sunscreen everyone else forgot?

Start paying attention to the work you gravitate toward, especially when things are unclear or no one's quite sure what to do next. That's often when your truest strengths emerge—not because someone assigned you a role, but because you stepped into it instinctively and executed with impact.

Those spontaneous contributions are among the most reliable indicators of your core strengths. They may not be part of your formal job description, but they're crucial to the functional role you play.

FEEDBACK

When I talk about feedback, I don't mean the annual review kind. I mean the type that comes from people who know what it's like to work with you, depend on you, or be led by you. One of the most powerful exercises I've ever used in coaching and team development is deceptively simple. It involves asking your peers to fill in the blanks of two sentences:

- What I admire about you is ________________.
- I'd come to you for help with ________________.

That's it. It's so simple, but you'd be amazed by what surfaces. Sometimes, people hear things they've suspected about themselves but never had confirmed. Other times, they're blindsided in the best possible way. I've watched seasoned professionals tear up when they realize that what they thought was just "how I do things" is actually the superpower their colleagues count on them to perform.

These moments matter. They shift the narrative. They give you new language for what you're good at and, just as importantly, what others see in you when you've forgotten to look.

In my Purpose-Driven Leadership Mastermind sessions, this exercise always sparks something bigger. Leaders start to see patterns. Maybe you're the one who always brings calm to a storm. Maybe you ask the questions no one else is brave enough to ask. Maybe you show up with structure when things get chaotic, or you bring the energy when things get stuck.

Listen to how others describe you in annual reviews and formal exercises, but also in offhand comments. Are you the one they always come to when things get messy, or when they need a plan, or when they're stuck in their heads, or when they need to laugh?

Whatever it is, these patterns aren't just personal—they're portable. They go with you, from role to role, team to team, and season to season.

CAN'T NOT

Management thinker Peter Drucker used the wonderful double negative "can't not" to describe those core strengths we return to again and again. These are skills that may also be healthy compulsions. Maybe you can't not organize the chaos, speak up when something's off, or make peace between warring departments. Anything that's not destructive that you find almost irresistible is probably a strength.

There's a difference between how you *show up in the moment* and what you're wired to do over time. Both are clues to your strengths. If spontaneity reveals how you instinctively respond in a given situation, your "can't nots" show up across situations, regardless of your role, your title, or the task at hand.

Your strengths are throughlines. They don't just name what you do; they describe how you're built. They're not situational. They're structural. And that means something crucial when you're facing disruption: Skills are transferable.

SKILLS ARE TRANSFERABLE

Your job title, team responsibilities, or daily routine may all go out the window when disruption lands on your doorstep, but your strengths aren't going anywhere. Disruption may test your resilience, but it's also an opportunity to redeploy your strengths in a new direction or to solve new problems.

The same skill set that helped you manage a product launch can help you lead a community project. The intuition that made you a great mentor can help you navigate customer dynamics.

When you understand your core capacities, you can repackage them for new roles, reapply them to new challenges, and reassert them as tools for growth.

Here's how to start:

- **Name the pattern.** What's the core capability behind your past wins?

- **Translate the skill.** How could that capability serve in a different context?

- **Test the fit.** Where can you pilot this strength in a small way to create impact?

The people who grow through disruption don't leave behind what made them great in their old life; they take it with them and find new ways to use it in their new one.

THE ENGINEERING MINDSET

Applying your strengths with precision, especially under pressure, turns potential into performance. When you understand not only what you're good at but also how your strengths interact with different environments, you're able to deploy them to maximum effect.

     DISRUPTED

As an example, let's say you instinctively sort complexity into structure. People often ask you to help them find the signal in the noise or make sense of multilayered issues. If it feels like that's just how your brain works, one of your core strengths is clarity. When you apply that talent intentionally, it becomes a superpower. You help teams align. You simplify the complicated. You bring focus and direction when things feel messy. In fast-moving or ambiguous situations, this strength shines. It calms the room.

But like all strengths, clarity has a shadow. Under pressure, the same instinct to organize can harden into a desire for control. That's not a failure of character, just the natural distortion of a strength under stress. (In fact, another method of finding your strengths is to look at the "shadow" side of "flaws.") Your strength of clarity, under stress, might lead you to shut down too early, push too hard for resolution, or dismiss perspectives that don't fit the structure you see.

You need a way to monitor how your strengths manifest and a plan for what to do when they go awry. Use this table to break each strength into its core components and start engineering it for impact:

Component	Definition	Prompt
Raw Talent	The instinctual response you bring to a challenge or opportunity	What do I reach for without thinking?
Strength in Action	The behavior this talent produces when consciously applied	When do I feel most effective and energized?
Stress Pattern	How the strength backfires under pressure or becomes a "saboteur"	What happens when I overuse or misapply this strength?
Redirection Lever	The internal shift or cue that restores alignment when things go sideways	What habit or mindset helps me recalibrate?

Completed for our example trait of clarity, it looks like this:

Component	Definition	Prompt	Actions
Raw Talent	The instinctual response you bring to a challenge or opportunity	*What do I reach for without thinking?*	I naturally seek to simplify, organize, and explain things in a way that makes sense. My first instinct is to cut through noise and highlight the essential.
Strength in Action	The behavior this talent produces when consciously applied	*When do I feel most effective and energized?*	I communicate vision or direction in ways that others can grasp quickly, translate complexity into clear steps, and ensure everyone is on the same page.
Stress Pattern	How the strength backfires under pressure or becomes a "saboteur"	*What happens when I overuse or misapply this strength?*	Under stress, clarity can become rigidity—oversimplifying, cutting people off, or being overly direct in ways that feel dismissive to others.
Redirection Lever	The internal shift or cue that restores alignment when things go sideways	*What habit or mindset helps me recalibrate?*	I can pause to listen deeply and invite others' perspectives. I'll remind myself that clarity is about creating *shared* understanding, not just advancing my version of it.

 DISRUPTED

Once you've engineered a few of your key strengths this way, you'll start to see patterns, not just in what you're good at but also in how, when, and why those strengths make an impact.

When you understand your strength system, you can help others clarify theirs. And when you understand the environmental conditions that support strengths, you can begin designing the environments of your team meetings, conversations, and cultures to make them places where innovation feels safer and strengths can thrive.

When you create that kind of space—first for yourself, then for others—you both perform and lead better.

READING + REPS

One strength and one stretch to engineer your strengths

At least once this week (and each day, if you're up for it), identify one of your core strengths and then find one slightly uncomfortable context in which to flex it. It's crucial to try using your strengths outside your comfort zone and in unfamiliar contexts, because doing so helps expand your range at a time when it's all too tempting to retreat into the familiar, where things feel safe.

For example:

- If your strength is strategic clarity, try applying it in a messy team discussion when the group is spiraling out of control. Instead of waiting to be asked, step in with a summary or structure.

- If your strength is empathy, apply it to someone outside your usual circle. It could be the quiet person on your team, a colleague who's been underperforming, or a stranger in the coffee shop.

- If your strength is humor, try bringing it into a high-stakes situation that feels tense and could use a little levity.

To help you track this growth over time, a simple weekly One Strength, One Stretch Tracker is below. Use this worksheet to apply one of your strengths in a slightly unfamiliar or challenging context each day. Reflect on how it felt, what impact it had, and what you learned.

Weekly One Strength, One Stretch Tracker

Day	Strength Applied	New Context (Stretch)	Confidence (1–5)	Impact (1–5)	Notes / Learning
Mon					
Tue					
Wed					
Thu					
Fri					

Strengths are skills that get stronger the more you use and stretch them. Applying a strength in a new context has three significant advantages:

1. You build range and realize that this part of you can travel further than you thought.

2. You build confidence, not because you nailed it, but because you showed up as yourself in a place that used to feel intimidating.

3. You also build better feedback loops. You start noticing what energizes you and seeing what lands with others. You start building the muscle memory to reach for your strengths, even under pressure.

If you stick with this process—even just for a week—you'll start to see yourself differently. You'll realize you're not waiting to become

     DISRUPTED

a better leader, because you're already leading; with each passing day, though, you're just doing it more consciously.

And that's the shift: not from weak to strong, but from unconscious to intentional.

ENGINEERING YOUR STRENGTHS

It's our natural inclination, amplified by the negativity bias, to focus on correcting our deficiencies. The counterintuitive truth is that the only way to bring out our best is to focus more on honing our natural strengths. When disruption hits, it's easy to feel like the version of yourself that was capable, creative, and confident has vanished. But it hasn't. It's just buried under noise, fear, and the frantic search for what's next.

Your strengths don't get erased by change. They're not tied to a title, a team, or a season of life. They're yours—they are you. If you're willing to identify them, apply them intentionally, and stretch them creatively, you'll both perform and feel better.

PART 3

LIFT OTHERS AS YOU RISE

CHAPTER 9

BE VULNERABLE

A few months after I launched Whitman Consulting, my young mentee Caleb and I ran into Jerry, a fellow Virginia Military Institute alum. Caleb introduced us, and I asked Jerry a sales-related question. He launched into a ten-minute master class that left me so energized I hugged him. When I got home, I looked him up online and understood why his advice had landed with such impact: Jerry was recognized as one of the top five salespeople in the world.

The very next week, I received my first request for proposal (RFP) from a potential client and was unsure how to price it. After a moderate amount of agonizing, I swallowed my pride, picked up the phone, and asked Jerry for guidance. I told him the price I was considering, and he didn't hesitate. "Double it," he told me. "Then add $900."

The next day, terrified but trusting Jerry's advice, I slid the proposal across the table. I expected the client to balk or at least negotiate. Instead, he scanned the numbers, nodded, and said, "Looks good." Just like that, my first contract was signed—and at double the price I would have asked for on my own. It only happened because I was willing to be vulnerable enough to ask for help.

Later, when I called to thank Jerry, I asked why he'd been willing to help me. His answer has stayed with me ever since. He said he'd seen the time I'd invested in Caleb, and that had told him everything he needed to know about my value as a consultant.

In the previous three chapters, we explored embracing uncertainty, connecting with purpose, and discovering your strengths. These personal shifts are vital, but they're only half the story. The next stage of growth is relational and turns personal growth into collective momentum.

Our capacity to navigate disruption and reach meaningful success directly relates to our ability to build trust. Without trust, we are confined to what we can accomplish alone, with little ability to delegate effectively or form strong partnerships with others. Trust-building, however, is not an innate trait—it is a learnable skill that can become a true superpower in leadership.

Disruption often forces us into new territory, requiring us to both learn from and lead people we may not yet know. In those moments, our instinct is usually to protect ourselves by staying guarded and focusing on whom not to trust. The counterintuitive truth is that trusting first by being vulnerable is the key to inspiring people to trust us. In turn, they're more likely to be willing to go the extra mile in helping us achieve our goals. To trust first is to lead.

WHY WE GUARD OURSELVES IN DISRUPTION

When disruption hits, most people shut down or close themselves off. This isn't a matter of personality or a moral failing. It's biology. Research in affective neuroscience shows that when the brain perceives uncertainty or danger, it activates the amygdala and hypothalamic-pituitary-adrenal (HPA) axis, triggering physiological responses that extend beyond fight or flight and into social withdrawal and reduced exploratory, social, and trusting behavior.[31] In other words, at precisely the moment when we need each other most, our neurochemistry becomes more risk-averse, less empathetic, and less likely to engage in prosocial actions.[32]

For many leaders, this impulse shows up as guardedness. We pull back from others to avoid exposing our doubts and double down on control. It may seem like the smart play to try to manage perceptions, protect credibility, and get through the chaos with as little exposure as possible. But that instinct often slows down progress or even backfires.

What feels protective to you may look like isolation to others, and in the context of disruption, isolation can be toxic. It breaks down teams, slows decision-making, and creates a risk-averse, reactive environment that undermines team adaptability and innovation.[33] Ironically, in trying to maintain control, we often lose connection, and without connection, we lose influence.

CONTROL MAY MAKE PEOPLE COMPLY, BUT VULNERABILITY MAKES THEM COMMIT.

---

31   Naomi I. Eisenberger and Steve W. Cole, "Social Neuroscience and Health: Neurophysiological Mechanisms Linking Social Ties with Physical Health," *Nature Neuroscience* 15, no. 5 (2012): 669–74, https://doi.org/10.1038/nn.3086.

32   Ming Hsu et al., "Neural Systems Responding to Degrees of Uncertainty in Human Decision-Making," *Science* 310, no. 5754 (2005): 1680–83, https://doi.org/10.1126/science.1115327.

33   Gemme D'Auria and Aaron De Smet, "Leadership in a Crisis: Responding to the Coronavirus Outbreak and Future Challenges," McKinsey & Company, March 16, 2020, https://www.mckinsey.com/capabilities/people-and-organizational-performance/our-insights/leadership-in-a-crisis-responding-to-the-coronavirus-outbreak-and-future-challenges.

When a leader shares what they're struggling with, admits what they don't know, or simply says, "This is hard for me, too," it signals humanity—and humanity is magnetic. Vulnerability, as Brené Brown's research has shown, is a fundamental building block of trust. People trust leaders who are relatable, emotionally available, and consistent.[34] A leader's vulnerability invites others to show up fully. Once they do, real collaboration becomes possible.

WHAT VULNERABILITY IS

I remember working with a senior leader whose team had just been through a round of layoffs. He was showing up late to meetings and giving short answers, and he was visibly checked out. At first, I thought it was just burnout, until I knocked on his door and asked how he was doing. He paused. Then he said, "I feel like I failed." He had invested everything in that team, and now that things were falling apart, he didn't know how to show up anymore.

I didn't try to fix the situation. I just sat with him in that space, but that moment of vulnerability changed us both. He no longer seemed unapproachable to me, and as he started opening up and connecting more, his remaining team members followed his lead.

Vulnerability means sharing something both real and risky. That might mean admitting a mistake or asking for help. It might be telling your team, "This project matters to me, and I don't have all the answers yet." Or it might be saying to someone, "I've been avoiding this conversation, and that's on me."

---

34   Brené Brown, *Daring Greatly: How the Courage to Be Vulnerable Transforms the Way We Live, Love, Parent, and Lead* (Gotham Books, 2012), 45.

THE NEUROSCIENCE OF VULNERABILITY

Research by Paul Zak, a pioneer in neuroeconomics, shows that acts of vulnerability stimulate the release of oxytocin, the "O" in the neurochemical acronym DOSE from Chapter 4, which is associated with bonding, generosity, and cooperation.[35] In a fascinating twist, this release occurs not only in the person being vulnerable but also in those who witness the vulnerable act. That biochemical response triggers the impulse to empathize, protect, and cooperate, a phenomenon psychologists refer to as "affiliative behavior." In other words, when we witness someone take an interpersonal risk, our brains become more inclined to reciprocate than retreat. This is how one act of courageous openness can cascade into a culture of trust.

But oxytocin isn't triggered by mere exposure. It's triggered by risk, which is why authenticity matters. When we're overly polished or rehearsed, people may admire us, but they won't necessarily trust us. Trust begins when people sense that we're being real, when they see us stretch beyond what's comfortable to offer something honest, uncertain, and human.

LEADERSHIP IS MORE ABOUT BEING REAL THAN BEING RIGHT.

Zak's research suggests that this neurochemical cascade is a biological reward for mutual vulnerability. It's the body's way of reinforcing cooperation and connection. When we share something real, it becomes easier on the neurochemical level for others to

---

35   Paul J. Zak et al., "The Neurobiology of Trust," *Annals of the New York Academy of Sciences* 1032 (2004): 224–27, https://doi.org/10.1196/annals.1314.025.

meet us in that space. Vulnerability isn't just a social signal. It's also a physiological one. And when we create environments where it's safe to show up with that kind of openness, we go beyond changing behavior; we change brain chemistry.

I've seen team sessions where people were holding back, watching each other, and waiting to see if it was safe to speak up. Then, someone shared something personal—not dramatic, just honest. Other people started leaning in, nodding along, and adding their own stories in what Harvard organizational behaviorist Jeff Polzer calls a "vulnerability loop."[36]

These loops start when one person shares something emotionally meaningful. If the other person responds with care, empathy, or even a small act of openness, the loop closes and the brain releases oxytocin, deepening social bonds and trust.

WHY BE VULNERABLE?

When a leader shares what they're struggling with, it gives the team permission to stop pretending. They stop wasting energy managing impressions or guarding their insecurities and get more honest, more creative, and more committed.

Vulnerability is a gateway to relationships grounded in trust, shared humanity, and mutual commitment. When you let people see the real you, you create space for them to bring more of themselves to the table. That's the starting point of a relationship that

---

36   Daniel Coyle, "How Showing Vulnerability Helps Build a Stronger Team," TED, Feb. 20, 2018, https://ideas.ted.com/how-showing-vulnerability-helps-build-a-stronger-team/.

can weather disruption, disagreement, and difficulty—and come out stronger on the other side.

That kind of relationship pays dividends far beyond the moment of disruption. The longest-running study on human well-being found that the strongest predictor of lifelong happiness and health isn't wealth, status, or achievement; it's the quality of your relationships. People who feel securely connected handle stress better, stay mentally sharper, and live longer. And while that research wasn't focused exclusively on workplace happiness, its lessons apply here. Authentic relationships buffer you from the more destructive aspects of disruption.[37] They're also the basis of psychological safety.

WHY PSYCHOLOGICAL SAFETY IS IMPORTANT

Our behavior is far more context-dependent than we tend to realize. Social psychologists have shown that even the most capable and thoughtful person can struggle to contribute when the system around them sends the wrong signals. In high-safety environments—where people feel respected, accepted, and free to speak up without fear of embarrassment or retaliation—creativity and collaboration spike. Teams take more intelligent risks, and learning accelerates. But in low-safety environments, even top performers tend to go quiet. They avoid conflict, suppress their instincts, and second-guess their contributions. They haven't suddenly forgotten how to perform; the conditions just no longer support it.

---

37   Evelyn F. Acoba, "Social Support and Mental Health: The Mediating Role of Perceived Stress," *Frontiers in Psychology* 15 (2024): https://doi.org/10.3389/fpsyg.2024.1330720.

A recent McKinsey study found that 85 percent of executives believe fear is holding back innovation in their organizations. That statistic didn't shock me. But you know what did? Ninety percent of those same organizations are doing nothing about it.[38]

In other words, most leaders recognize that fear is a problem, but they still don't actively create environments where people feel safe enough to try something new. And what is true on the organizational level shows up inside each of us. Our individual fears—of failure, embarrassment, or loss of control—shut down our creativity.

It's the now-familiar amygdala hijack story playing out again, and the solution is essentially the same: We need to create an environmental DOSE. In any space we create where it's safe to experiment, whether for ourselves or for our teams, strengths begin to surface. New ideas start to emerge, and the full range of talent finally has room to breathe.

HOW TO LEAD WITH VULNERABILITY

In times of disruption, relationships can either fracture or deepen, and the difference often comes down to whether you're willing to go first. Going first means being human before being polished. It means sharing something real, asking the hard question, or reaching across the silence with a gesture of trust. That choice is never without risk, but it's always a step toward something stronger.

---

38   Laura Furstenthal et al., "Fear Factor: Overcoming Human Barriers to Innovation," McKinsey & Company, June 3, 2022, https://www.mckinsey. com/capabilities/people-and-organizational-performance/our-insights/ fear-factor-overcoming-human-barriers-to-innovation.

The irony of vulnerability is that it feels like exposure, but it creates safety. When we lead from a place of self-trust, guided by intention and shaped by a willingness to connect even when it's uncomfortable, we create the conditions for others to do the same.

For me, the choice to lead with vulnerability starts with self-awareness. I try to check in with myself regularly, especially after meetings or high-stakes conversations, to gauge whether I was being real or performing. Sometimes, I realize I avoided saying what I actually thought to prevent conflict or because I was worried about being judged. Those moments don't feel huge, but over time, they shape how we show up. If we're not intentional, they can quietly pull us away from the kind of leadership we want to practice and the kind of relationships we want to have.

One habit that has helped me is a connection scan. Once a day, I ask myself, *Who did I really connect with today, and where did I hold back?* If I notice a pattern, I pay attention to it. If I keep avoiding a particular conversation or person, I dig into why. The act of noticing is sometimes enough to shift the dynamic. And of course, one of the most powerful things a leader can do is to own their missteps. When you miss the mark, say so—not defensively or with an explanation, just honestly. Try saying, "I mishandled that. Here's what I'm learning, and here's how I want to move forward." That kind of repair builds trust faster than any polished presentation.

BUILD SAFETY FROM THE INSIDE OUT

Vulnerability is risky by definition. When you open up to someone, you're trusting them with something soft, unguarded, and real. Most of the time, that risk pays off. But when it doesn't, you need to know that it won't break you. Leading others with vulnerability starts on the outside, but it only works when it's anchored on the inside.

There's a kind of strength that comes from knowing you can face a challenge, feel its full weight, and still move forward. That kind of internal security comes from an internal signal that says, *I'm solid here. I don't have to prove myself to you, because I've already proven something to myself.*

Because your credibility, influence, leadership, and ability to build trust with others will never exceed the amount of trust you've built with yourself, self-trust is both a prerequisite for vulnerability and the source of its power. When you're anchored in your values, you don't need to perform confidence; you're just confident. You can risk going first. You can trust others not because it's safe but because you're strong enough to handle the disappointment if they let you down.

Leaders who cultivate inner safety show up differently. They don't need to dominate a room to feel secure. They don't confuse control with influence, and they're not easily thrown off course by pushback or discomfort. That steadiness makes them magnetic. It's easy to trust them because they're not trying to prove anything; they already trust themselves.

HOW TO CULTIVATE SELF-TRUST

Self-trust isn't binary. It waxes and wanes, and most forms of disruption take a toll on it. When unforeseen events shake your world, it's hard not to doubt yourself or, at the very least, your predictive abilities. But self-trust can be rebuilt when it starts to crumble. Here are a few simple practices that will help you restore or strengthen your trust in yourself.

KEEP SMALL PROMISES

Keeping small promises to yourself is one of the most underrated habits that builds confidence and self-trust. If you promise yourself you'll do something—whether it's to wake up early, go for a walk, or not eat the rest of the pie—keep your word. If you know you can count on yourself to keep your commitments, you'll be both more in charge of your life and more trustworthy.

If you find yourself prefacing your goals or plans with phrases like "I'll try to" or "I want to," it may indicate that you've let yourself down before and are hedging your bets against future disappointments. Be as scrupulous with your promises to yourself as you are with those you make to other people. If you find it difficult to say you're going to start exercising without adding "try to," consider making a more modest promise that you're confident you'll keep. If you regularly practice making and keeping promises to yourself, even if nobody knows you're doing it, you'll seem more trustworthy to others.

AUDIT YOUR ACTION

Periodically ask yourself if you're living your values. The goal isn't guilt—it's clarity. These audits help you course-correct before the drift becomes a divide. Of course, it's hard to act from your values if you haven't articulated them. So, if you didn't do this work in Chapter 2, take time now to write down the principles that matter most to you. Then, look at your week and ask: *Where are these showing up? Where are they not?*

OWN YOUR OOPSIES

Nothing reinforces trust with yourself (and others) like owning a misstep and taking action to fix it. It's also one of the most honest forms of vulnerability. When you admit without defensiveness or deflection that you've made a mistake, you're choosing honesty over ego.

Don't wait until it's safe. This particular form of vulnerability is most powerful when it happens in real time, not after the dust has settled. A quick "Hey, I messed up, and I want to make it right" can do more to build trust than a dozen flawless performances. It shows you're humble enough to be honest, mature enough to take responsibility, and invested enough to put in the work to repair any damage done. It also builds credibility. People will be more likely to take your word for something, knowing you're willing to revise it when needed.

CELEBRATE THE SMALL WINS

Notice those moments when you do the hard thing, follow through, or show up well. Acknowledging the many times you don't let yourself down strengthens your faith in your ability to act with courage and consistency. It also reinforces the behavior neurologically.

As we discussed in Chapter 4, each time you recognize a small win, your brain releases the reward and motivation neurochemical dopamine. That small hit of dopamine doesn't just feel good; it teaches your brain to keep going, to keep choosing the hard thing, to keep showing up with integrity. This is especially important during times of disruption, when motivation can dip and progress feels ambiguous. In those moments, celebrating effort rather than waiting for uncertain outcomes keeps the momentum alive.

Keeping small promises to yourself, auditing your actions, owning your oopsies, and celebrating small wins all send the message to yourself that you're paying attention and taking responsibility for how you show up. You'll start believing you're dependable, and when that message gets internalized, it becomes much easier to offer trust to others and to ask for it in return.

TRUST THROUGH TENSION

It's tempting to think that trust means keeping the peace and that an absence of overt conflict is a sign that interpersonal dynamics are healthy. Often, the opposite is true. High-trust environments can be quiet and peaceful, but more often, they're not. The true indicator isn't the absence of conflict but the presence of candor.

Some of the most transformative moments I've witnessed in teams and partnerships didn't come during periods of ease. They came during difficult, honest conversations where people said what they'd been holding back, named what others were dancing around, or risked asking a question that might not land well.

That's where vulnerability becomes leadership.

There's a kind of trust that only emerges after tension has been addressed rather than avoided. When we step into those moments with care and curiosity—not to confront, but to connect—we show that the relationship can hold truth, not just harmony.

When I'm coaching leaders through complex dynamics, I often invite them to use what I call the "gentle opener," something like these:

- "Can we talk about something that's been on my mind?"

- "I might be off base, but I'd rather ask than assume."

- "I'm bringing this up because I care about our work together."

Those kinds of sentences create room for hard truths without triggering defensiveness. They lower the temperature, signal intention, and invite dialogue rather than debate.

Conflict avoidance is easier in the short term, but it's unsustainable. Only when we engage—vulnerably, respectfully, and clearly—can we build relationships that get stronger over time. When people know they can disagree with you and still be respected, they feel more at ease. They become braver and trust you more.

So, the next time something feels off, don't wait for it to blow over. Try naming it. Ask the question. Say the thing. Those moves aren't easy, but they build trust.

THE VULNERABILITY FRAMEWORK

Vulnerability isn't about oversharing or dramatics; it's about signaling humanity, openness, and shared imperfection in ways that invite others to do the same. This framework organizes nine practical demonstrations of vulnerability into three dimensions to create a practical guide for using everyday moments to build trust.

DIMENSION 1: HUMAN CONNECTION

Vulnerability begins with showing you're more than a role—you're a person:

- **Open with a story.** Ground the room in something real from your life. Sharing a personal story signals that the human side matters.
- **Open with curiosity.** Ask check-in questions that invite authenticity. Go first with your own answer to show that openness is safe.
- **Name the good.** Call out what you genuinely admire or appreciate in others—be specific and say it out loud.

DIMENSION 2: COURAGE IN THE MOMENT

Trust grows when leaders risk honesty in real time:

- **Name the unspoken.** When tension is present, bring it into the light by acknowledging what others may be feeling but not saying.

- **Offer appreciation for risk, not just results.** Recognize the courage it takes to ask a question or speak up—even if the outcome isn't perfect.

- **Model recovery.** When you stumble, own it quickly. Restate what you meant, and show that mistakes are part of growth.

DIMENSION 3: SHARED GROWTH

Vulnerability also means sharing purpose and accepting help:

- **Share your "why."** When making a request or giving feedback, reveal the motivation behind it. This transparency deepens trust because it lets people know where you're coming from.

- **Let yourself be helped.** To demonstrate that collaboration matters more than pride, ask for support with something you could do alone.

- **End with reflection.** Close by naming what you've learned or what stuck with you. Reflection models humility and shows you've truly listened.

You don't need to do all nine at once. Choose one practice from each dimension—connection, courage, or growth—and weave it into your next meeting. Over time, these small acts create a culture where trust is not just built but multiplied.

READING + REPS

Nine easy ways to build authentic connections

Relationships don't deepen by accident. They grow when you show up on purpose. This week, choose one of the nine practices from the Vulnerability Framework and commit to trying it for the next five days. Track how it changes the quality of your conversations and your sense of connection.

All nine are small things, but they build the connective tissue teams and partnerships thrive on. The key to each of them is simple: Go first. Extend the kind of trust, presence, and openness you'd like to receive. That's what creates the conditions for others to do the same.

BEING VULNERABLE

When you lead with openness, you create the conditions for real connection. You stop performing and start relating. And in that shared humanity, trust takes root.

We instinctively guard ourselves, especially when the world feels uncertain. But the leaders who earn trust aren't the ones who build walls. They're the ones who go first, show who they are, and, in doing so, give others permission to take similar risks.

In disruption, people don't expect you to have every answer. They just want to know you're human and will face the storm with them. That's what builds safety, earns loyalty, and turns individual growth into lasting, resilient relationships.

CHAPTER 10

CARE ABOUT OTHERS

Several years ago, when my division of Lockheed Martin went through a massive reorganization, I thought I knew how to keep things moving. My plan was simple: I'd identify quick wins, assign ownership, and deliver results that would reassure my boss we were on track. It seemed like the right play, and on paper, it was. But it didn't work.

I asked one of my most capable team members, Judy, to drive a critical project. She had the experience and insight to be successful in the role, yet no matter how often I shared that this would be great for her career and encouraged her to step up, she wouldn't take it on. Week after week, I pressed harder, convinced that clearer expectations and better understanding would do the trick.

Then, almost in passing, my assistant told me something I hadn't known. Judy was in the middle of a painful divorce. Suddenly, her reluctance made sense. It wasn't disengagement but exhaustion. She was living through an extreme personal disruption.

So, I tried a different approach. In our next meeting, I didn't ask about the project. I simply asked, "Are you okay?" She looked stunned, then began to cry. What followed wasn't a conversation about metrics or deadlines. It was a conversation about loss, resilience, and the fear of falling so far behind that no one would believe in her again. She wanted to move the project forward to advance her career, but she'd lost her confidence. I told her I believed in her, and I told her why.

Two weeks later, she took on that project and turned it into one of the most visible early wins of the reorg.

Leading through disruption isn't about tightening your grip when things get shaky. It's about loosening it to allow room for people to be humans. Instead of control, it's about care.

It's natural to want people to get on board with whatever you're building. At the most fundamental level, that's the purpose of businesses and their leaders: coordinating people to accomplish what one person can't on their own. But stories of visionary leaders demonstrate that the most effective path to alignment isn't to force people to help you reach your goals; it's to first fully understand theirs. When your focus aligns with theirs, you can build together. If it doesn't, you can move on with clarity and respect. Either way, authentic leadership is rooted in care.

It's our natural intuition to get people on board with what we want them to do for us. The counterintuitive truth is that the most effective way to get buy-in is first to understand what they need and see if it aligns with what we want; if it does, we can then coordinate our efforts to achieve joint success.

INDUSTRIAL AGE MANAGEMENT

In the early days of management theory, when work was primarily physical and repetitive, stability and predictability were the goal. You didn't need emotional intelligence to run a factory line. You needed compliance, consistency, and a clean chain of command. Frederick Winslow Taylor, one of the world's first management consultants, espoused a "scientific management" model in the early twentieth century that treated workers almost like extensions of machinery, subordinate to the system they worked within.

Managers were glorified, while workers were interchangeable and optimized for efficiency. "In the past, the man has been first; in the future, the system must be first," as Taylor put it. "In most cases, one type of man is needed to plan ahead and an entirely different type to execute the work."[39]

For much of the twentieth century, this mindset shaped how organizations operated. Even into the postwar corporate boom, leadership remained essentially positional. Movement up and down the corporate ladder was obvious, with authority, respect, and pay increasing progressively. A person's influence came from the title they held. Tenure equated to loyalty and was rewarded. Climbing over people on the way up was part of the game. Caring about an "underling's" values and goals would have seemed odd. (Thinking of them as "underlings" would not.) A manager wasn't responsible for workplace culture or employee engagement; they just needed to keep the machine running.

INFORMATION AGE MANAGEMENT

With the rise of the knowledge economy and increasing globalization, the assumptions that held together the old command-and-control systems unraveled. A new class of workers, whom Peter Drucker dubbed "knowledge workers," were increasingly in demand and valued for their insight, not their output.[40]

---

39   Frederick Winslow Taylor, *The Principles of Scientific Management* (Harper & Brothers, 1911), 7 and 34.

40   Peter F. Drucker, *Landmarks of Tomorrow: A Report on the New "Post-Modern" World* (Harper & Row, 1959).

Their best work couldn't be extracted through oversight. It had to be invited through trust.

As management structures flattened and the pace of change accelerated, predictability disappeared. Leaders were no longer just managing productivity; they were navigating complexity, volatility, and human dynamics. In such environments, transactional relationships began to break down, and the shift from managing people to collaborating with them began.

Recent research confirms that as AI adoption rises, organizations place an even greater premium on emotional intelligence, adaptability, relationship-building, and ethical reasoning.[41] As we increasingly build and lead hybrid teams of humans and machines, the need to understand human collaboration becomes foundational.

THE NEUROSCIENCE OF LISTENING

Humans are a social species, and our brains are social organs. We're biologically wired not only to enjoy one another's company but also to depend on it for our survival. For most of human history, being ostracized from the group didn't just hurt a person's feelings; it threatened their life. Our brains evolved to pay close attention to social cues about who was safe, who wasn't pulling their own weight, and who was likely to help if things went sideways.

41   Workday, "New Global Research from Workday Reveals AI Will Ignite a Human Skills Revolution," news release, Jan. 14, 2025, https://newsroom. workday.com/2025-01-14-New-Global-Research-from-Workday-Reveals-AI-Will-Ignite-a-Human-Skills-Revolution.

In fact, a theory popular in evolutionary biology suggests that the human brain evolved specifically to detect lies through a combination of cognitive and emotional responses—that's how fundamental trust (and its absence) is to us. Oxytocin does much of the heavy lifting here. Released in moments of connection—especially when we feel seen, heard, or supported and during acts of generosity—it plays a central role in how humans build trust, even in high-stakes environments.[42]

This means that leaders build trust by creating the kinds of interactions that *feel* safe, where the nervous system relaxes in its warm oxytocin bath. And few ways of interacting do that more powerfully than sincere and attentive listening.

Interestingly, oxytocin doesn't just spike in the person who feels listened to; it also increases in the listener. That means when you practice authentic listening and genuinely tune in to what someone else is saying, both of you get a neurochemical payoff.

Of course, this kind of deep listening takes energy, presence, and intention. But when you do it well, it doesn't just make the other person feel good. It changes the brain chemistry of the interaction itself, creating space, lowering the emotional temperature, and opening the door to new possibilities.

When people feel understood, they tend to loosen their grip on their defenses and stop spending energy managing appearances or protecting their egos. That frees them to contribute more fully, take risks, and be creative. Collaboration replaces competition.

---

42   Michael Kosfeld et al., "Oxytocin Increases Trust in Humans," *Nature* 435, no. 7042 (2005): 673–76, https://doi.org/10.1038/nature03701.

This means that when you create a safe environment as a leader, you gain access to more of people's brilliance.

THE ALCEA METHOD OF HUMAN-CENTERED COLLABORATION

As a leader, you can't leave showing that you care about people to chance. It needs to be structured. It may sound strange to plan acts that are typically spontaneous, but spontaneity is, at best, erratic. A flexible, adaptive structure creates consistency, and consistency builds trust.

With this in mind, I developed the ALCEA Method as a coaching tool. I wanted a simple, repeatable way to help leaders shift from directive to collaborative conversations, especially when tensions were high or trust was fragile. Over time, it evolved into a framework for building connections in almost any context, from team meetings and mentoring conversations to cross-functional partnerships—and even those awkward coffee chats where both people feel a little unsure of the script.

Each letter of ALCEA represents a move rather than a step, as they don't need to happen in perfect order. Together, these moves shape a way of engaging that turns ordinary interactions into something more meaningful.

A — ASK

Start with curiosity rather than with your plan or opinion. Asking open-ended questions, especially those starting with "what" or "how," signals that you're coming to the interaction looking for more than the desired outcome that prompted it.

Example Open-Ended Questions:

- What's been on your mind lately?

- What are you most looking forward to in the coming quarter?

These questions aren't likely to create too much of a digression, but they will likely spark a few minutes of conversation. That's the point. Spending those agenda-free minutes in this way demonstrates respect and can reveal what people care about most, before you ever try to influence them.

L — LISTEN

I'm not talking about the kind of half-present, checking-your-phone kind of listening we're all familiar with. That won't do anything to foster the relationship you're trying to build, only damage it. Quiet your internal commentary long enough to truly take in what's being said. Pay attention to body language. Allow for silence. Most people aren't used to being listened to that deeply. When it happens, they feel it. And neurologically, as we saw earlier, so do you.

It can be painfully tempting for leaders to try to fix problems that may emerge, but focus on being purely receptive early in these interactions. If they raise an issue you want to address, you can always do so later. "I was thinking about something you said in our last conversation" is an excellent way to demonstrate both that you really were listening and that you care enough to think of them even when they're not around.

C — CLARIFY

Misunderstandings hide in assumptions. Clarifying means looping back, gently and with humility, to ensure you understand what the other person meant. Sometimes called "reflective listening," it can be as simple as using templates like these:

- "So what I'm hearing is…Does that sound right?"

- "Just to make sure I'm tracking—you're saying..."
- "Could you give me an example of..."

This step takes an extra beat, but it saves hours of confusion down the line. It also reinforces that you're processing and valuing their perspective.

E — EMPATHIZE

Empathy doesn't require you to agree with the other person's words or emotions, only to acknowledge them and pause long enough to feel with—not just for—the person in front of you. Sometimes that's expressed verbally:

- "That sounds like fun."
- "I can imagine that's frustrating."
- "If I were you, I'd feel the same way."

Sometimes it's expressed nonverbally with a breath, a shift in tone, or a moment of shared stillness. Showing empathy lets people know they're not alone in whatever they're experiencing. That alone can change someone's day.

A — ALIGN

This is where understanding moves into action. If you've been building rapport before moving to a predetermined topic, you can use alignment to ease the transition by pointing out shared goals, common values, and overlapping priorities.

If such an agreement is present, call it out. If it's not, don't force it. Ask alignment-finding questions like these:

- "Where do we want the same things?"
- "What would a win look like for both of us?"

- "How can we move forward in a way that honors what matters to you and what matters to me?"

When you find alignment, you can build momentum. When you don't, you can part ways respectfully and with clarity, not conflict.

You don't need to memorize the acronym. You already know how to do these things. ALCEA is a structure to return to when the conversation gets tense or slippery, and it's a tool for deepening ordinary interactions.

It's also useful in times of personal change or professional disruption, when the usual rules of social engagement shift.

NAVIGATING SOCIAL DYNAMICS AFTER DISRUPTION

It's one thing to build reciprocal relationships when you're in your groove, your role is clear, and your energy is high. Connection flows more naturally when life is stable. You have the time, the confidence, and the context to invest in relationship-building.

But disruption changes all of that. Whether it's a job loss, a leadership transition, a major life event, or even a quiet internal shift that reorders your priorities, disruption unsettles the dynamics you've relied on. When titles shift, the tempo changes, and the people who used to be in a close orbit start to drift, the usual way we've built relationships in the past no longer works.

This is where many people get stuck, not because they don't care about connection, but because they don't know how to reenter it from a new perspective. The old roles no longer fit, and the new ones aren't yet fully formed. So we hesitate. We ghost. We retreat into our uncertainty. If the disruption has shaken our confidence, we may even feel a certain amount of shame or embarrassment and want to hide. In other words, we feel vulnerable. And that, as we've already discussed, is a time of powerful opportunity.

Disruption disrupts routine conversation and strips away pretense. It gives us a chance to connect on a deeper level and invites us to move from role-based relationships ("You're the boss; I'm the direct report") to values-based ones ("We both care about growth, purpose, or impact").

That shift doesn't happen automatically. It takes intention, courage, and sensitivity to reach out to others when they've been disrupted (or when we have). The ALCEA moves—especially listening, empathy, and alignment—will help here, but they need to be applied with even more care.

During transitions, people are often carrying more than they show. Their energy may be lower and their confidence shaky. The assumptions they once relied on may no longer apply. This is when perspective-taking becomes a superpower.

The loss of a job often means the loss of an entire network of relationships, but it doesn't have to. If you're willing to show up differently and invite others to do the same, you might find that the strongest connections aren't the ones that come ready-made with the job but rather the ones you rebuild with empathy, alignment, and care after they are disrupted.

WHEN YOU'RE THE ONE WHO'S BEEN DISRUPTED

The ALCEA Method isn't only for leaders supporting their teams through disruption; it's just as valuable when you are the one navigating disruption. In fact, moments of personal transition are when this model becomes most personally challenging and most transformative.

Reaching out can feel vulnerable. When your identity is in flux or your confidence is wavering, asking for help may feel risky. You don't want to seem needy or burn relationship capital. You may not want to say, "I'm lost," even if that's exactly how you feel. Use the ALCEA Method to ground yourself.

Ask with humility and clarity. You don't need a polished pitch; it's enough to say:

- "I'm in the middle of a transition, and I'd really value your perspective."
- "I'm rethinking what's next, and you came to mind as someone who navigates change well."
- "I'm exploring some next steps and would love to hear how you've approached similar moments in your career."

When your request is human and specific, most people are more than willing to help. Remember, vulnerability promotes affiliative behavior.

Listen deeply. When someone offers you their time, treat it like a gift. Resist the urge to fill space with justifications or explanations. More than ever, allow for silences. Let them speak. Be curious and take notes.

Clarify to keep the conversation real. If you're unsure what someone means or if a suggestion doesn't quite sit right, ask a question:

- "Can I ask what that looked like in practice?"
- "I want to make sure I understand what you're saying. Is it..."
- "When you say…what does it mean for you day to day?"

This keeps the conversation from drifting into vague encouragement and demonstrates that you're engaged and deeply interested.

Empathize with the other person too! Even when you're asking for help, remember the quote widely attributed to Robin Williams: "Everybody you meet is fighting a battle you know nothing about."

Respect their boundaries, thank them for their time, and honor the fact that they took the time to be with you. You're not the only one in transition. Sometimes, your openness will give them permission to embrace change as well.

Align your next step. Whether or not this person is the one who can help you, ask yourself:

- *What just got clearer for me?*
- *What insight or phrase will stick with me after this conversation?*
- *What was the impact of their listening on me?*

Use these questions to help you craft a meaningful thank-you that builds alignment. Afterward, if there's a way to build a bridge—whether it's a follow-up, a collaboration, or a simple expression of appreciation—build it.

Reaching out to someone can be an invitation that says, "I'm in motion. I value what you know. And I'm showing up with care, even as I'm figuring things out." That's not weakness. That's leadership too.

READING + REPS

Five ways to build and sustain reciprocal networks

Reciprocal relationships are built over time, in ordinary moments, through engaged listening, thoughtful questions, timely follow-ups, and a willingness to trust. You don't need a formal initiative or a team retreat to start cultivating them. You just need a few intentional practices, repeated consistently. Some of the most effective ones are below.

1. PRACTICE A POSTURE OF OTHERNESS

Before each conversation (especially the hard ones), pause and ask yourself what the other person might be thinking and feeling. What are they hoping for in this exchange? What might they be worried about? This subtle mental shift primes your brain for empathy. It helps loosen the grip of your agenda and assumptions, while tuning your attention toward the other person's reality.

2. ASK "WHAT" AND "HOW" QUESTIONS MORE THAN YOU TALK

There's plenty of time for you to make your request or share your perspective, so start by soliciting theirs. Open-ended "how" and "what" questions create space for agency and can unlock insights that lead to better outcomes for both of you.

3. TRACK ALIGNMENT OPPORTUNITIES AND FOLLOW UP

If someone shares a goal, a need, or an interest that aligns with your work, write it down and follow up on it. Doing so doesn't take long, but it demonstrates that you're someone who listens, remembers, and helps.

4. NORMALIZE CAREER CONVERSATIONS

You don't need a formal performance review to check in on someone's growth. A quick one-on-one over coffee can go a long way, especially if it's grounded in genuine curiosity, rather than evaluation.

Ask things like:

- What would make this next stretch feel meaningful for you?

- Is there something you've been wanting to try that you haven't had the chance to?

- Where do you feel most energized right now? What drains you?

Even if you can't grant every request, the act of asking matters. It signals that you see them as a person with potential, not just a doer of tasks.

5. MAKE CARE VISIBLE

The smallest gestures sometimes carry the most weight. Try a quick note of encouragement, a public shoutout, or a follow-up message to say, "I heard you" or "I'm thinking about what you said." When done authentically, these expressions of concern create trust that extends far beyond the moment itself.

Leadership lives in these moments—not just in strategy meetings and speeches, but in hallway chats, Slack threads, and Monday check-ins. If you want to build a lasting network, don't wait for the perfect opportunity. Reciprocal relationships grow when we show up with curiosity, lead with care, and stay open to what's possible between us, not just what's possible *for* us.

CARING ABOUT OTHERS

Disruption doesn't just shake up systems; it reshapes relationships and challenges the way we connect, collaborate, and lead. In times of change, it's tempting to retreat into a command-and-control style of leadership, to try to rally buy-in by sheer force of will, or to retreat and lick our wounds. But people can't pitch in if they don't know there's a need. Either way, they engage most fully when they feel seen.

Shifting from the industrial leadership model built on extraction to one built on reciprocity affects all our interactions and matters even more when the ground is moving beneath our feet. It's the difference between "Here's what I need from you" and "What are you working toward—and how can we build something together?" The ALCEA Method is a simple but profound approach to listening, aligning, and leading with care that will help you connect with others and cultivate relationships that are both supportive and self-renewing.

It's our natural intuition to get people on board with what we want them to do for us. The counterintuitive truth is that the most effective way to get buy-in is first to understand what they need. If it aligns with what we want, we can then coordinate our efforts to achieve joint success.

Throughout this book, I've said that disruption, while uncomfortable, can also be a growth catalyst. Chapter by chapter, we've built a path from internal resilience to external influence. Here, in the realm of relationships, we find one of the most powerful accelerators of all: the ability to lead in reciprocal networks. When disruption hits, you need more than a plan—you need people you trust and who trust you in return.

In the next chapter, we'll explore what it means to scale that kind of leadership and foster systems, cultures, and environments where reciprocal relationships are the engine of progress. But it starts here, with genuine care for others practiced daily and deliberately, in part because once you understand what the people you lead truly want—their goals, fears, and motivations—you gain a powerful opportunity to align your aims with theirs. When your team sees how their personal aspirations advance the shared mission, ownership naturally follows. That sense of shared purpose transforms accountability from something imposed to something embraced. Instead of pushing for results, you create the conditions where people pull *themselves* forward—because success now feels like theirs too.

CHAPTER 11

INSPIRE ACCOUNTABILITY

Not long ago, I worked with two nonprofit cofounders who were facing a difficult stretch. Their organization had recently lost two program managers in a matter of months. Having just hired a third, they were worried about team cohesion and its ripple effect on performance.

What impressed me was that rather than blaming the employees who had left, the cofounders chose to look inward. They started by coming to me for leadership training for themselves, demonstrating that culture begins at the top. From there, we brought the full team together for cohesion work—clarifying roles, aligning on expectations, and talking openly about how each person preferred to give and receive feedback.

Finally, we implemented an accountability system that everyone could own. We introduced a simple RACI tool (responsible, accountable, consulted, informed) and paired it with open conversations about feedback preferences. Suddenly, execution became smoother, deadlines were clearer, and the daily frustrations began to fade. Over time, not only did the new program manager stay in place—longer than the past two combined—the whole team also began performing at a higher level, with less friction and more efficiency.

It's our natural intuition to think we need to hold people account-able by punishing them for not doing what we want or need. The counterintuitive truth is that the most effective way to get others to do what we want is to plant seeds of ownership in them—by doing our part first and then removing resistance to support them in doing theirs.

In Chapter 2, I introduced the 4-A Self-Leadership Loop, in which accountability (the third "A") means owning your choices, even when the results aren't what you hoped for. That's the mindset of accountability applied to your life. In Chapter 3, I explained the 1440 Method as a form of structural accountability for aligning the daily actions of your life with your deepest values. Those chapters focused on the mindset and execution system of personal ac-countability. This chapter scales those ideas and applies them to the shared goals and structures of team execution.

WIRED TO INSPIRE

Conventional wisdom says holding people accountable means tightening the screws. But the real work of leadership isn't about compliance; it's about commitment. Unlike compliance, commit-ment can't be coerced or enforced. It can only be inspired.

Many leaders I've worked with shy away from the idea of inspir-ing others. I believe it's one of leadership's core responsibilities, but I understand my clients' reluctance. They think the ability to inspire has something to do with personality, charisma, or extro-version. It feels almost mystical, when in fact, it's the most practi-cal thing in the world. Inspiration is simply leading by example. It's simple, but far from easy, because it means our job as leaders is to be worthy of imitation. When we visibly lead ourselves—demon-strating what it looks like to take ownership, act from our values, and build habits that don't rely on willpower—we plant seeds of ownership in others.

This isn't idealism. In the early 1990s, researchers studying primates discovered mirror neurons. These brain cells fire not only when we perform an action we've seen others do, but also when we simply observe them doing it. Scientists believe these mirror neurons underlie our capacity for imitation, empathy, and social learning.[43] If you've ever heard a parent (or yourself) say, "Do as I say, not as I do," you've experienced the frustration of running up against this kind of deep neural programming.

Long before humans had complex spoken language, we relied on modeling to pass down survival knowledge. So when we talk about modeling ownership, we're not just setting an example— we're tapping into a deeply embedded learning system. Leadership becomes contagious because the brain sees it as behavior worth mimicking.

Children have never been very good at listening
to their elders, but they have never failed to imitate them.
—James Baldwin

This is why modeling accountability is the sixth of the seven accelerators. We've laid the groundwork: You've stabilized yourself in uncertainty, clarified your purpose and strengths, and built strong connections with others. Now, it's time to model the behavior that

---

43   Giacomo Rizzolatti and Laila Craighero, "The Mirror-Neuron System," *Annual Review of Neuroscience* 27 (2004): 169–92, https://doi.org/10.1146/annurev.neuro.27.070203.144230.

makes those connections resilient and scalable, by reframing what accountability means and how it interacts with disruption.

REDEFINING ACCOUNTABILITY

Most people dislike the word "accountability." They associate it with shame and punishment, and no wonder. In many organizations, accountability has become code for blame. Holding someone accountable sounds like holding them over an open fire.

Unfortunately, somewhere along the line, the ideas of accountability and ownership got conflated and confused. Leaders "hold people accountable" in an attempt to force them to take ownership of their work and its outcomes. They want the people who work for them to be as invested in the company's success as they are. (Profit sharing and bonuses are other ways leaders try to increase ownership.)

However, the truth is that the most effective way to encourage ownership doesn't come from external pressure, whether positive or negative. It comes from buy-in. It sounds so simple. When people buy into something, they take ownership of it. Trying to force people who haven't bought in to take ownership will encounter the same resistance as any assault on their autonomy.

**PEOPLE DON'T RESIST ACCOUNTABILITY—
THEY RESIST BEING CONTROLLED.**

The more you micromanage, the more you erode trust and autonomy. According to the SCARF model developed by neuroscientist David Rock, people experience threats to their status, certainty, autonomy, relatedness, or fairness as real neurological stressors—ones that activate the brain's threat circuitry and release cortisol, narrowing attention and reducing cognitive flexibility.[44] When that threat response is triggered, creativity, empathy, and problem-solving—all essential to learning and growth—tend to shut down. The brain becomes defensive, reactive, and focused on the short term. This is, of course, the same response it has to disruption.

When ambiguity is high and direction is scarce, people rarely turn to a binder of instructions or guidelines—they look to their leader for signals of danger or safety. Your behavior is the signal. The first person you need to hold accountable is you.

DEMONSTRATE OWNERSHIP

You start creating a sense of ownership (and thus, accountability) in others by modeling it yourself, but I've seen too many leaders confuse accountability with oversharing. Perhaps in a bid to be seen as humble or self-effacing, or perhaps because they have yet to address their internal saboteurs, they cross the line from authentic to awkward.

Authentic accountability owns outcomes.

Accountable leaders acknowledge mistakes and take responsibility: "I missed the signal on this one. That's on me, and here's how I'm going to make sure it doesn't happen again."

They don't undermine their own credibility: "I guess I completely misread the situation. Honestly, maybe I'm not the right person to be making that call."

---

44   David Rock, "SCARF: A Brain-Based Model for Collaborating with and Influencing Others," *NeuroLeadership Journal* 1 (2008): 1–9, https://davidrock. net/portfolio-items/scarf-a-brain-based-model-for-collaborating-with-and-influencing-others-vol-1/.

Authentic accountability centers on solutions.
Accountable leaders move quickly from ownership to action: "We fell short on the launch, but we've mapped the gaps and have a plan to fix them this quarter."

They don't dwell on failure: "We really dropped the ball here, and I can't stop thinking about how badly we executed."

Authentic accountability empowers others.
Accountable leaders model responsibility that also invites others to step up: "I missed my part here. And I want each of you to look honestly at where we can all tighten things up."

They don't leave the team demoralized: "We really screwed up, and if something doesn't change, I can't see how we'll stay afloat."

Authentic accountability draws healthy boundaries.
Accountable leaders own their part but not everyone else's: "I should have set clearer expectations. That's on me. The missed deadlines, though, are on each of us to address."

They don't heap all the blame for everything on themselves: "At the end of the day, every failure rolls up to me, so if something went wrong, that's 100 percent my fault."

Authentic accountability is grounded and constructive.
Accountable leaders give feedback that's specific and growth-focused: "The report missed key data points. Let's walk through how we can build a better review process next time."

They don't frame feedback as personal disappointment or humiliate others: "This isn't to the standard I expect from us. We should all be embarrassed by how this turned out."

Authentic accountability strengthens trust.
Accountable leaders build credibility and safety through honesty:
"I know I let the team down this time. You deserve better, and I
intend to deliver it."

They don't question their team's ability: "If this is the best we can
do, I'm not sure how we'll earn the trust of our customers."

**Authentic accountability balances humility
with authority.**
Accountable leaders combine vulnerability with confidence: "I
made a call that didn't pan out. That happens. What matters is we
learn fast and adapt."

They don't use self-criticism to manage perception: "Maybe my
instincts aren't as sharp as they used to be. I clearly missed something everyone else saw."

These differences aren't always obvious on the surface. The most
dangerous misuse of accountability often hides behind language
that sounds humble, responsible, or driven by high standards. But
subtle choices in tone and framing determine whether accountability builds trust or corrodes it.

WHY DEMONSTRATE OWNERSHIP?

When a leader demonstrates authentic ownership of their actions,
words, and approach, it disarms the room. People start self-re-
flecting instead of deflecting. They shift from obligation to alignment and feel safe enough to step up, not because the leader
demanded it but because they set the example. I've seen it play out
dozens of times.

This isn't just anecdotal. In his foundational research on social
learning theory, psychologist Albert Bandura demonstrated that
people learn new behaviors not only through instruction but

also by observing others and internalizing the consequences of their actions.[45] When leaders model integrity, adaptability, and follow-through, those behaviors become socially contagious. In other words, your example is more powerful than your KPIs or compensation structure.

This is the business reason for all the work you've done on yourself:

- Your ability to embrace uncertainty becomes their permission to grow.

- Your commitment to putting "why" over "what" becomes their sense of purpose.

- Your focus on strengths becomes their confidence to contribute.

- Your willingness to share with vulnerability becomes their willingness to trust.

- Your demonstration of genuine care becomes their aspiration to do their best.

This is where private discipline becomes public credibility—and credibility is what gives leadership its power, because the only kind of accountability that scales is the kind you demonstrate.

RELY ON A STRONG SYSTEM

In Chapter 3, we established the 1440 Method as your personal execution system for aligning your daily actions with your deepest values. Now, we're going to scale that same principle—creating systems that remove resistance and enable execution—to your team.

---

45   Albert Bandura, *Social Learning Theory* (Prentice-Hall, 1977), 22–28.

The 1440 Method isn't about optimizing every second or running your life like a military drill. It's about creating an intentional schedule that nudges you toward what matters. A blocked calendar, a recurring reflection prompt, or a whiteboard that tracks progress can become a kind of inanimate accountability partner—quiet, steady, and impossible to argue with. With each significant new disruption, revisit the 1440 Method to see what needs to adjust:

- Re-clarify your intentions with a fresh completion of the Life Wheel.
- Reevaluate and reset your SMARTI goals based on what you're inspired to pursue next.
- Refill your average perfect day with inspired actions that align with your new direction.
- Reestablish your habits using the iceberg framework to make your new behaviors automatic.

The real payoff of having a system like the 1440 Method in place is that it creates the conditions for small wins, which generate the motivation to keep going. And importantly, that's the correct ordering of wins and motivation. We don't get motivated and then go out and win.

ACTION CREATES MOTIVATION.

Across social psychology, clinical trials, and goal-pursuit research, initial action reliably creates or amplifies motivation. When internal cues are weak, people infer their attitudes from their own actions—"I did it, so I must be the kind of person who does this." Small initial acts increase willingness to take larger related actions later. In clinical settings, behavioral activation—the simple prescription to *act first*—matches the effects of full cognitive behavioral therapy for depression and performs comparably to antidepressant medication in severe cases.

The mechanism is straightforward: Action produces identity inferences ("I'm the kind of person who does this"), reduces cognitive dissonance (attitudes shift to match behavior), creates reinforcement loops (visible progress fuels more action), and removes friction through automation. Daily progress on meaningful work is the single strongest driver of motivation and engagement.

This is why your system matters. You may not always have a supportive boss or a high-performing team, but you'll always have yourself. It's how you choose to lead yourself, especially in the quiet, structureless, or newly structured seasons, that determines how you'll lead others.

TEAM SYSTEMS

Having modeled ownership via your own behavior and maintained your personal execution system through disruption, you're able to extend the same principles to your team. The goal isn't to replicate your exact 1440 Method for everyone else but rather to create the conditions where others can take ownership of shared goals.

Instead of barking orders or hovering over progress bars, disruption-tested leaders do three things differently: They define outcomes, design systems, and give forward-looking feedback.

Disruption-tested leaders answer one question that shifts everything: *What does "done" look like?* Clearly defined outcomes both align expectations and give people the autonomy required for ownership. And autonomy, as the SCARF model reminds us, is a core driver of motivation. When people understand the goal and feel trusted to reach it, they rise to the occasion.

Disruption-tested leaders design low-friction systems that make follow-through easy. This might mean shared dashboards, visible milestones, or standing check-ins that focus on progress and learning rather than blame and pressure. The goal isn't to watch people like hawks but to reduce ambiguity, remove resistance, and make ownership feel natural.

These systems work for the same reason your personal 1440 Method works: They automate decisions, reduce friction, and create visible progress. When teams can see their wins accumulating, motivation compounds. When the path forward is clear, people don't need to be pushed. They pull themselves forward.

Just as your personal system helps you act regardless of your motivation level, team systems help your people start moving before they feel fully ready. And that action generates its own momentum.

A well-designed accountability system makes ownership visible, follow-through consistent, and communication transparent. At its core, every strong system shares four elements:

1. **Clear Roles and Expectations**
   Having identified what the desired outcome looks like, a good accountability system defines each team member's part in getting to "done." Everyone knows what they own, where their authority begins and ends, and how their decisions connect to the larger mission.

2. **Goals and Metrics**
   Shared objectives are aligned with organizational priorities and measured by clear outcomes—KPIs, OKRs, or another simple scorecard that keeps purpose front and center.

3. **Schedule and Monitoring**
   Regular check-ins—weekly meetings, one-on-ones, or quick stand-ups—keep work visible and allow for course

corrections before small issues grow large. Tools like Asana, Trello, or Jira help track commitments and progress without micromanagement.

4. **Consequences and Recognition**
    Accountability cuts both ways. When commitments slip, the leader is more coach than critic. When goals are achieved, the leader celebrates and reinforces the behaviors that got the team there. Both responses strengthen the culture of ownership.

Systems like these translate your team's intentions into consistent habits, turning accountability from an abstract ideal into a daily practice.

Finally, disruption-tested leaders deliver feedback differently. People won't always get it right. They'll miss deadlines and drop the ball. Leaders who demonstrate ownership meet those moments with a grounded presence, modeling what it looks like to course-correct without shame and giving their team permission to do the same.

The accountability of others often comes into play when someone has not performed the way we would like. It typically sparks the question "Can I give you some feedback?"—which triggers the average person in a negative way.

It's common for people to feel nervous, anxious, or defensive when they hear this question, which creates a barrier to communication and prevents them from receiving the feedback constructively. Worse, sensing this disconnect, many leaders either double down on the intensity of their feedback or abridge what they intended to say out of concern over being too harsh.

In either scenario, the effectiveness of the conversation diminishes, growth stalls, and shared goals are put at risk. In disrupted states,

   DISRUPTED

trigger sensitivity is heightened, so it's especially important to pay attention to these emotional nuances.

Disruption-tested leaders see these conversations as potential catalysts to unlock the hidden growth and talent in each team member and keep their feedback focused on the future.

FEEDBACK WITH FORESIGHT

Whereas traditional feedback tended to be either harsh or vague and focused on the unchangeable past, forward-looking feedback concerns itself with what might be different in the future.

This approach draws from Marshall Goldsmith's concept of "feedforward," in which leaders provide specific direction on how to improve in the future rather than rehashing what went wrong in the past.[46] By shaping performance conversations toward specific outcomes in the future, you reduce anxiety, increase motivation, and unlock potential people didn't even know they had.

Here's how to give feedback with foresight:

1. **Check intentions.** Before you speak, ask yourself: *Am I focused on the best interest of what I need done AND what the person needs?*
2. **Shift the lens.** Instead of focusing exclusively on what went wrong, also pay attention to what they *can do right* moving forward.
3. **Determine the win.** Visualize what success will look like if this course correction works.

---

46   Marshall Goldsmith, "Try Feedforward Instead of Feedback," accessed Dec. 5, 2025, https://www.marshallgoldsmith.com/post/try-feedforward-instead-of-feedback.

4. **Be kind and clear.** You don't have to be harsh, but you do have to be completely clear about expectations. Clarity is kindness.

5. **Follow through.** Do your part by establishing a rhythm to check on progress and sticking to it. Make tweaks as needed as you go.

With this simple shift, you may be able to tap into a level of talent in your team that no other leader ever has. When leaders add foresight to feedback, performance conversations stop being purely about mistakes and start considering possibilities.

READING + REPS

Daily, weekly, biweekly, monthly and ad hoc ways to move accountability from a concept into regular practice

1. OWNERSHIP AUDIT (FIVE MINUTES DAILY)

Strengthen the habit of self-accountability before expecting it from others.

At the end of each workday, reflect on three questions:

1. *Where did I follow through on what I said I'd do today?*

2. *Where did I fall short, and what can I do differently tomorrow?*

3. *What signal did my behavior send to my team?*

Write down brief answers—one or two sentences each—and track patterns over time.

Why it works: Daily reflection builds self-awareness and reinforces the link between intention and action.

2. MODEL THE MISS (WEEKLY OR AS NEEDED)

Practice visible ownership of mistakes, and model constructive accountability.

In your next team meeting, share one decision or action you wish you'd handled differently. Name the impact it had, outline what you're doing to correct it, and invite others to reflect on how they might improve their own processes.

Why it works: Publicly taking responsibility normalizes learning from mistakes and encourages others to do the same.

3. THE "DONE" DEFINITION DRILL (WEEKLY)

Clarify expectations and empower autonomy.

Before delegating a task or starting a project, write out a one-sentence definition of what "done" looks like. Share it with your team, and ask them to refine or challenge it. Revise together until everyone agrees.

Why it works: Shared definitions reduce ambiguity, increase ownership, and align everyone around the same outcome.

4. SYSTEM TUNE-UP (BIWEEKLY)

Make accountability easier by removing friction.

Review one recurring process or workflow with your team (e.g., weekly check-ins, project tracking, feedback loops). Ask, "Where do things get stuck? What could we automate, clarify, or simplify?" Then, implement one small improvement.

Why it works: Consistent iteration builds systems that sustain accountability without micromanagement.

5. GIVE FEEDBACK WITH FORESIGHT (WEEKLY)
Build skill in giving feedback that fuels growth rather than fear.

Choose one person each week to give forward-looking feedback to, using this structure: "Here's one thing I think would make an even bigger impact next time…" Remind them to keep their focus entirely on the future, not the past.

Why it works: Regular forward-focused feedback builds trust, reduces defensiveness, and creates a culture of continuous improvement.

6. ACCOUNTABILITY AGREEMENTS (MONTHLY)
Turn shared ownership into shared practice.

Host a short team session to review commitments and update responsibilities using a RACI chart or similar tool. Ask each person to state one specific action they'll own in the coming month. Record these publicly, and revisit them in the next session.

Why it works: Public commitments increase follow-through and make accountability a collaborative process rather than a top-down demand.

7. MIRROR MOMENT (ANYTIME DISRUPTION HITS)
Reset accountability in uncertain times.

When circumstances shift or momentum stalls, pause and ask:

1. *What's still within my control?*
2. *What action can I take today, even if it's small?*
3. *What example do I want to set in how I respond?*

Why it works: This simple pause transforms uncertainty into intentional leadership action.

Over time, if you practice leading yourself first, building trust and ownership in your teams, and designing systems that sustain progress even under uncertain conditions, these small, consistent actions compound, turning accountability into the cultural backbone of a team that grows stronger with every disruption.

INSPIRING ACCOUNTABILITY

Accountability begins with how you carry yourself and radiates outward. When you consistently demonstrate ownership, you give your team a living example of what responsibility looks like. Pairing that example with systems that make progress visible and achievable transforms accountability from an obligation into a shared commitment.

It begins with how you respond to challenges, adapt when circumstances change, and keep moving when no one is watching. It grows through the daily habits and structures you design to turn intention into results. And it becomes part of your culture when your actions give others the confidence to take ownership themselves.

When you model and support accountability in this way, it becomes self-sustaining. People begin to take initiative because they see its value. They match your follow-through with their own. They meet high expectations with creativity and care. Over time, this shared commitment turns teams into communities of trust, where people feel motivated by a sense of purpose and pride in their work.

Accountability is a leadership multiplier. It turns your individual integrity into your team's collective momentum. It builds the conditions where growth continues even when circumstances shift. And it prepares your organization for what comes next: the challenge of building adaptive systems that not only sustain accountability but allow it to evolve as the world changes.

CHAPTER 12

WANT TO BE WRONG

In the late 1800s, William Wrigley Jr. was just another salesman trying to carve out a living selling household goods, convinced that soap was his ticket to success. It wasn't going well. To drum up sales, he started offering a free tin of baking powder with every bar of soap. Soon, customers were coming to him for the "bonus" baking powder, treating his soap as an afterthought. Wrigley had believed in his soap, but he was willing to be wrong. He gave up on cleaning products and started selling baking powder instead.

He did better with baking powder than he had with soap, but unwilling to simply enjoy that win, he tried the same trick again, this time giving away sticks of chewing gum as a promotion. Once again, the freebie outshone the product. And once again, Wrigley pivoted—building one of the most iconic consumer brands in history.[47]

I used to think that the people who made it to the top were those with the brightest ideas and the best strategy for their execution, perhaps coupled with the most impressive degrees. As an engineer,

---

47   Nathan Aaseng, *Business Builders in Sweets and Treats* (Oliver Press, 2005), 43.

that explanation made sense to me. But over the years, working with leaders across disrupted industries, I've seen that long-term success isn't a function of intellect or education. The leaders who grow through disruption aren't the ones with the best answers. They're the ones with better questions.

It's our natural inclination to settle into our own point of view and to try to persuade others of its validity when conflict arises. The counterintuitive truth is that real, sustained success requires the courage to choose growth over comfort, to shift from conviction to curiosity, to update your mental model, to adapt your behavior to new circumstances, and to create structures for ongoing progress.

CHOOSE GROWTH OVER COMFORT

Bill Eckstrom, a leadership researcher, puts it like this: "Comfort and growth cannot coexist."[48] Growth happens only when we step outside familiar environments of predictability and into new zones of complexity. Complexity challenges our current skills and assumptions, which creates the friction needed to stretch. That stretch, sustained over time, drives transformation—not just in our performance but also, crucially, in our identity.

Most of us have been conditioned to see identity as fixed. We say things like "I'm not a people person" or "I don't do change well," without realizing we're limiting what's possible. In a disrupted world, having a fixed identity is a liability. What used to define you—your job title, your expertise, your industry—might not exist five years from now.

---

48   Bill Eckstrom, "Why Comfort Will Ruin Your Life," TEDx Talk, University of Nevada, Jan. 31, 2017, 12 min., 34 sec., https://www.youtube.com/watch?v=LBvHI1awWaI.

You can keep redefining who you are. The more you practice stretching into new environments, the easier it becomes to decouple your future from your past. At Whitman Consulting, we call this "identity flexibility." It's the ability to anchor yourself in your values while you reinvent potentially everything else about yourself. André 3000 from the hip-hop group Outkast took identity flexibility to its logical extreme, turning constant reinvention into his identity. Of course, I'm not suggesting you go out and learn to play the flute, but I'm also not telling you not to.

SHIFT FROM CONVICTION TO CURIOSITY

We all like to think of ourselves as open-minded. But the truth is, most of us are far more committed to our own perspective than we realize. It's easy to start believing your viewpoint is the correct one—maybe even the only one that makes sense—once you've achieved a certain amount of success and are in a position of leadership. When conflict shows up, the instinct is to convince, defend, or retreat.

Conflict, almost by definition, activates the amygdala and triggers the fight-or-flight response, derailing the part of the brain responsible for reason, empathy, and long-term thinking. In that state, personal growth seems secondary at best. Openness feels downright risky. Now is the time for a DOSE. If you can deliberately interrupt your stress response, you'll restore your capacity to lead from a place of presence instead of protection.

From there, it's much easier to recognize that the real work of leadership isn't to win the argument at all costs and convince everyone that your way is the right way. Yes, conflict is uncomfortable, but since discomfort is required for growth, every difference of opinion is an opportunity to grow. Learning to move toward conflict with curiosity, rather than retreating from it or charging in to win, is what separates adaptive leaders from rigid ones.

When you approach disagreements with the intention to learn rather than win, you give yourself the chance to grow into someone you couldn't have become on your own. Research on intellectual humility shows that people who score high on intellectual humility are more likely to engage with opposing viewpoints, ask clarifying questions, and update their beliefs in response to new information—all of which are crucial for leaders operating in rapidly changing environments.[49]

I use a simple framework adapted from the work of Amy Gallo to help teams understand and engage in healthy conflict.[50] First, determine which of three kinds of conflict you're experiencing—task, process, or relationship:

- Task conflicts are disagreements about *what* should be done.
- Process conflicts are disagreements about *how* it should be done.
- Relationship conflicts are disagreements about *who* should do it.

Task and process conflicts can be generative when handled well. Relationship conflicts, on the other hand, tend to derail growth

---

49   Tenelle Porter and Karina Schumann, "Intellectual Humility and Openness to the Opposing View," *Self and Identity* 17, no. 2 (2017): 139–62, https://doi.org /10.1080/15298868.2017.1361861.

50   Amy Gallo, *HBR Guide to Dealing with Conflict* (Harvard Business Review, 2017), https://store.hbr.org/product/hbr-guide-to-dealing-with-conflict/10068.

because they shift the focus from ideas to personalities. The three types represent the difference between "That's the wrong thing to do," "That's the wrong way to do it," and "You're wrong."

As a leader, if you can shift the focus from relationships to tasks and processes, you will more easily access the kind of healthy creative tension that fuels better thinking. That only happens, though, when there's enough psychological safety for people to challenge ideas without fear of the conversation getting personal.

One exercise I use is a structured debate in which participants argue both sides of an issue. For example, in one recent session, I assigned half of the group to argue that AI development should accelerate, while the other half argued that it should be halted entirely. Then, we switched sides. What made this exercise powerful wasn't just the topic but the experience of advocating for an assigned, rather than chosen, position. It forced participants to listen differently. It gave them a visceral understanding of what it feels like to question their assumptions and represent a worldview they may not hold. And it's an excellent set-up for the persuasion trifecta.

A PERFECTED TRIFECTA

We often teach the *persuasion trifecta* as a tool for influencing others. Aristotle identified three essential elements of a compelling argument: ethos, pathos, and logos, i.e., credibility, emotion, and logic. Since our goal isn't to persuade others of our perspective but to learn more about theirs, we can turn these tools inward and use them to deepen our listening.

To listen through all three channels, ask yourself:

- *Who is this person and where are they coming from?* (ethos)
- *What are they feeling, and why does it matter to them?* (pathos)

- *What reasoning or experience is shaping their point of view?* (logos)

This kind of listening expands your mental map. It can help you recognize things you hadn't noticed, question what you took for granted, and learn from perspectives you might otherwise dismiss. After all, you can't grow by listening only to echoes of your own thinking. You grow by listening through the discomfort to ideas that challenge your beliefs, feelings, and reason.

When you stop needing to win and start wanting to understand, you develop a kind of clarity that's only available on the other side of curiosity. You stop seeing conflict as a threat and start seeing it as a signal that something here matters. If people are upset, it means they care. If you're upset, you've found something important. Either way, there's something you need to learn.

With this expanded view, it is much easier to facilitate a resolution to any conflict. Often, seeing an issue from multiple perspectives will help you reach a new solution. By taking the lead and truly listening first, you break the dam of conflict. People are much more willing to listen once they feel heard.

UPDATE YOUR MENTAL MODEL

We all navigate the world through internal maps we've built to make sense of how things work. These "mental models" form the underlying framework that shapes what we pay attention to, how we interpret information, and which choices feel obvious or inevitable. Leaders rely on these models every day, often without realizing it, to guide decisions, set priorities, and connect cause to effect.

Updating your mental model is one of the most important disciplines in a world defined by disruption. It begins with a willingness to consider perspectives beyond your own, but it doesn't end there. You also need to step back and analyze how the world itself has changed.

Start by examining the problems your purpose aims to solve. Are they still the same, or have they shifted in scale, scope, or shape? Sometimes, the core issue remains, but the conditions around it have evolved, demanding new methods and tools. At other times, what was once the central challenge has been replaced by something entirely different.

In either case, sticking to an old mental model risks irrelevance. As you adapt, ask yourself two critical questions: *Where are the opportunities that didn't exist before? How are we uniquely positioned to take advantage of them?* Disruption doesn't just close doors; it opens new ones. Leaders who consistently update their mental models are the ones who spot those openings early and accelerate through them with clarity and confidence.

ADAPT HOW YOU ACT

Adaptability is the engine behind high performance under rapidly shifting conditions. Research by the US Office of Personnel Management, later expanded by Elaine Pulakos and her colleagues, gives the name "adaptive performance" to this ability to handle emergencies, learn new tasks quickly, and adjust to unpredictable work situations. The results indicate it's one of the strongest predictors of long-term job success across a wide range of roles and industries.[51]

---

51   Elaine Pulakos et al., "Adaptability in the Workplace: Development of a Taxonomy of Adaptive Performance," *Journal of Applied Psychology* 85, no. 4 (2000): 612–24, https://doi.org/10.1037/0021-9010.85.4.612.

It's tempting to wait until you feel ready to start adapting your actions to fit changing circumstances, but mindset often follows motion. The highest-performing leaders I've coached don't wait for clarity before they act. They run experiments on themselves and prototype new ways of thinking and acting.

Because tiny adaptive actions practiced regularly form the bedrock of behavioral flexibility, I encourage clients to treat it like any other muscle. You don't lift the heaviest weight on day one. You lift something light, consistently, and build from there. That might mean trying a different communication channel, delegating a task you usually own, or brushing your teeth with your nondominant hand.

I'm not trying to downplay how extremely challenging the need to radically change familiar behavior patterns can be. Learning to adapt your behavior to new circumstances can feel overwhelming, especially for those of us who built our identities on technical mastery or strategic precision. In stable environments, it makes sense to focus on optimization, predict what's coming, build the right systems, and repeat what works. But we no longer live in that kind of environment. The systems keep changing, the roles evolve, and the rules get rewritten halfway through the game. Because disruption is the most reliably predictable occurrence, adaptability is the skill to optimize and growth systems the right ones to build.

SYSTEMATIZE ONGOING GROWTH

To a certain extent, this book is itself a system for ongoing growth: The seventh accelerator, *want to be wrong*, brings us right back to the first, *embrace uncertainty*. Over the years, I've come to see growth as something to be not just pursued but designed. If you want to keep evolving as a leader, you need systems that make it easier to stretch, notice, and shift. Without such structures, even the most ambitious leader tends, under pressure, to revert

DISRUPTED

to survival mode. One client of mine put it perfectly: "If I don't schedule my growth, I do something easier. Like kettlebells."

At Whitman Consulting, we help people build structures that make ongoing learning an integral part of their lives, from the quiet to the disrupted and back again. One senior leader I worked with started treating her weekly calendar like a laboratory. She picked one behavior a week, such as how she gave feedback, led meetings, or handled conflict, and treated it like a controlled experiment, testing out new models, theories, or practices.

Your structure doesn't need to be elaborate; it just needs to be a structure. It could involve setting a new intention every Monday morning or taking five minutes to reflect each Friday. Try asking your team once a month what you're not seeing or introducing a challenging question at your next family dinner. What matters is the repetition—small practices compound.

One strategy I often recommend to clients is the weekly reframe. Take a moment at the end of each week to look back at something that frustrated or challenged you. Write an account of what happened, what you thought, how you felt, and the actions you took. Then, ask yourself what other thoughts you could have had and how you would have subsequently felt and acted as a result. Is the story you told yourself the only possible one? What else might be true?

Perhaps the most underrated growth habit is seeking feedback. Unlock new insights by asking questions like these:

- "What's one thing I'm missing?"
- "Where did I make things harder than they needed to be?"
- "What would you do differently if you were in my shoes?"

If asked weekly as part of your ongoing growth structure, they can be truly transformative.

Studies by psychologists Wendy Wood and David Neal suggest that habit-based behaviors operate below the level of conscious awareness; however, when paired with intentional goals—such as daily reflection or weekly reframing—they can reshape behavior and the underlying identity that drives it.[52] In other words, who you are becomes a function of what you routinely practice—or, as Aristotle put it more than two thousand years ago, "We become just by doing just acts, temperate by doing temperate acts, brave by doing brave acts."[53]

That's not just true at the individual level. Whole cultures can be built to systematize ongoing growth and respond to disruption by getting stronger rather than falling apart. As I mentioned in Chapter 5, Nassim Nicholas Taleb calls this quality "antifragility." Antifragile systems improve in the face of stress and treat volatility not as a threat to avoid but as a source of strength to cultivate. Taleb points to examples in biology, where muscles rebuild stronger after resistance. In business, antifragile teams reflect, adapt, and reconfigure under stress to outperform more rigid ones. Antifragile leadership cultures encourage experimentation, reward learning from setbacks, and build structures that thrive on feedback. They're not built to survive disruption—they're built to improve because of it.[54]

READING + REPS

---

52   Wendy Wood and David Neal, "A New Look at Habits and the Habit–Goal Interface," *Psychological Review* 114, no. 4 (2007): 843–63.

53   Aristotle, *Nicomachean Ethics*, trans. Terence Irwin (Indianapolis: Hackett Publishing, 1985), 1103a.

54   Taleb, *Antifragile*.

Five daily adaptation exercises

Big changes often start with small choices. If adaptability is a muscle, these exercises are the push-ups. They aren't meant to transform your life in a single sitting. They're designed to create the conditions where growth becomes your default setting. Use them to build agility into your routines, even on ordinary days when everything goes as planned.

1. LISTEN IN THREE DIMENSIONS

The next time you find yourself in a disagreement, try listening through the lenses of ethos, pathos, and logos. Ask yourself:

- *What does this person's background or credibility tell me about why they think what they do?*

- *What emotions or unspoken concerns might be shaping their response?*

- *What logic are they using, and where does it differ from mine?*

The goal isn't to replace your way of seeing with theirs but rather to stretch your mind far enough that it can encompass a different point of view. When you get in the habit of listening to understand instead of listening to win, you build the kind of perspective-taking ability that makes growth possible in moments of tension.

2. TRY ON A DIFFERENT PERSPECTIVE

Pick a topic that triggers you. It doesn't have to be political or high-stakes, just something about which you have a strong opinion. Spend five minutes writing or talking from the opposite viewpoint—not as a devil's advocate, but as if you genuinely believed it. Force your mind to search for logic, emotion, and credibility in that argument.

It's extremely unlikely those five minutes will change your beliefs, but they might loosen your grip on them enough to see what else might be true. That slight widening of perspective, no matter how uncomfortable, is the essence of adaptation.

3. DEBRIEF A MISTAKE WITHOUT JUDGMENT

We're taught to move on from mistakes quickly, but speed can lead to skipping over learning. Once a week, choose a moment when something didn't go the way you'd hoped, and instead of judging or justifying, interrogate it. Ask yourself:

- *What assumption did I bring to the situation?*
- *What signal did I miss?*
- *What pattern does this remind me of?*
- *What new option is now visible because of this experience?*

Mistakes don't teach you anything unless you take the time to learn from them.

4. SCHEDULE AN EXIT FROM YOUR COMFORT ZONE

Every week, block time for something that stretches you. It doesn't have to be public or dramatic. It could be reaching out to someone whose work you admire, offering a bold idea in a meeting, or saying no when you usually say yes. Over time, these small doses of discomfort build your tolerance for uncertainty. And in an unpredictable world, that tolerance is gold.

5. END THE DAY WITH A QUESTION

Before bed, ask yourself, *What did I get better at today?* Some days, the answer will be obvious. Other days, it might be subtle. On hard days, the answer might be: *I practiced showing up even when I didn't feel like it.* That still counts.

This daily reflection reinforces the identity shift at the heart of this chapter. You are not just someone reacting to a disrupted world. You are someone learning to grow, intentionally, every day.

WANTING TO BE WRONG

Adaptability means responding with wisdom, not speed. It means staying curious in the face of uncertainty, testing new possibilities instead of relying on old assumptions, and expanding your perspective when the situation calls for more than your current point of view.

ADAPTABILITY IS THE NEW STABILITY.

Leaders who thrive in a constantly changing environment treat adaptability as a core practice. They pay close attention to what's shifting. Consequently, they see emerging patterns earlier than their peers. They build teams that grow stronger under pressure and cultures that evolve by deliberate design.

It's our natural intuition to hold tightly to our perspectives, especially when we're chasing achievement. But real, sustained, exponential growth requires the courage to challenge our assumptions, stay open to conflict, and continually adapt.

Each wave of change presents an opportunity to lead with greater awareness, precision, and impact. One of the most powerful ways to take advantage of that opportunity is to look for the places where you might be wrong. A posture of intellectual humility and open-minded curiosity unlocks the door to learning, supports better decision-making, and creates an environment for your teams to improve as well.

AN INVITATION

Disruption doesn't wait for permission, and it doesn't end when the chapter does. If anything, finishing this book is less a conclusion than an invitation to move forward with greater clarity, deeper resilience, and a steadier hand in the face of change.

At the heart of *Disrupted* is a simple truth: Disruption isn't a detour on the path to growth—it *is* the path. Whether it arrives as a job loss, a business pivot, a personal crisis, or a global shock, disruption doesn't just shake up your circumstances. It shakes up your sense of identity, direction, and control. But if you're willing to engage with it, if you can stop resisting the chaos and start learning from it, disruption can become your most powerful teacher.

In Part 1, you built a foundation for that kind of disruption-driven transformation by learning how to lead yourself through instability. You picked up some tools to manage your time and energy with intention, regulate your mental state, and interrupt the internal narratives that keep you reactive. These stabilizing skills are the deeply rooted structure that keeps you grounded when everything around you is shifting.

In Part 2, you stepped into the work of moving with purpose. You learned to adapt rather than reacting—and to stop waiting for clarity and start generating it through action. You developed the right mindset, defined your purpose, and engineered your strengths so that you could move into the next phase of your journey as a beacon of inspiration.

In Part 3, you turned outward. You explored what it means to show up with greater authenticity and impact—not by having all the answers, but by acting with vulnerability in alignment with what matters most. You learned to model the behaviors that build credibility and to practice the kind of leadership that not only survives disruption but actually transforms through it.

Disruption has a way of making us forget our own resilience. So if you're going through it now, remind yourself: You've done hard things before. You've faced uncertainty, made tough decisions, and rebuilt when things fell apart. This time is no different. You're not broken. You're becoming.

The counterintuitive and science-based truths in this book are designed to help you move through change in the most effective and enjoyable way. When we're convinced of the rightness of where we're going and why, and when we have techniques to bring out the best in ourselves and those around us, disruption becomes a joyful, adventurous journey.

Remember, motivation doesn't come before action; action *creates* it. The moment you take even the smallest step toward an important goal, your brain rewards you with the neurotransmitters to want to keep going. So, you don't need to have everything figured out to take that step. You just need to take it. Growth doesn't come from knowing. It comes from moving. Keep learning. Keep adjusting. Keep showing up.

And if you fall along the way or when the next storm comes—and it will—you'll know exactly what to do: Grow up.

ACKNOWLEDGMENTS

Writing this book has been one of the most clarifying experiences of my life. It forced me to distill years of lessons into something tangible—something that reflects not just what I've learned but also the people who helped me learn it.

I want to thank Jennifer LaMothe, who first asked me to share this book's content in a keynote four years before it was written. Thank you for lighting a spark that never went out.

I'm grateful for my wife, Myesha, the steady presence and partner who completes the other half of everything I am. Nothing in these pages would exist without your love, patience, and belief.

I want to thank my children, Alexis and Carter. Alexis, from the moment I saw you, my life found its greater meaning. You began my clarity on "why." Carter, born two weeks before Whitman Consulting began, you've been my living reminder of growth, possibility, and joy. Watching you "grow up" has been one of my life's greatest privileges.

I want to thank my sister, Angie, for her unwavering generosity and selflessness. You've always given without asking, loved without condition, and modeled grace in motion.

I want to thank my father, Whitman, who represents the foundation I still stand on today and who continues to stretch my thinking, even now.

I want to thank my book coach, Skyler, whose insight, questions, and curiosity helped me uncover the deeper truths within these pages.

I'm grateful to my mentor, Jerry Acuff, whose wisdom helped early in my entrepreneurial journey and has remained a steady source of support ever since.

A special thank-you to my clients for trusting me with their growth and their leadership journeys—you've allowed me to live out my purpose and reminded me why this work matters.

Finally, a heartfelt thank-you to my team at Whitman Consulting, my friends, and my extended family for the countless "micro- and macro-reps" that refined these ideas in real time: You are the living proof that leadership is learned not in theory but in relationship. This book is, in many ways, a reflection of all of you—your influence, your trust, and your belief that better leadership creates a better world. For that, I am endlessly grateful.

ABOUT THE AUTHOR

Andre W. Thornton is the founder and CEO of Whitman Consulting, one of the top ten leadership-development firms in the US, which helps organizations grow their people faster than their challenges.

A former engineering director at Lockheed Martin, Andre spent sixteen years leading teams on advanced aircraft programs and capturing over $1 billion in new business before discovering his true calling: developing leaders.

His book, *Disrupted*, introduces the two stabilizers and seven accelerators that turn chaos into growth—a framework drawn from neuroscience, engineering, and two decades of coaching experience.

Andre helps executives and teams raise their baseline, shorten recovery, and lead with clarity in times of change. He lives in Maryland with his wife, Myesha, and their two children.

Disrupted-Book.com